Earth Sciences

Earth Sciences

Curriculum Resources and Activities for School Librarians and Teachers

Amy Bain

Janet Richer

Janet Weckman

2001
Teacher Ideas Press
A Division of
Libraries Unlimited, Inc.
Englewood, Colorado

TEACHER IDEAS PRESS
A Division of
Libraries Unlimited, Inc.
P.O. Box 6633
Englewood, CO 80155-6633
1-800-237-6124
www.lu.com/tip

Library of Congress Cataloging-in-Publication Data

Bain, Amy J. (Amy Jo), 1958-
    Earth sciences : Curriculum resources and activities for school librarians and teachers / Amy Bain, Janet Richer, Janet Weckman.
       p. cm.
    Includes bibliographical references and index.
    ISBN 1-56308-678-6 (pbk.)
    1. Earth sciences--Study and teaching (Primary) 2. Earth sciences--Study and teaching--Activity programs. I. Richer, Janet. II. Weckman, Janet. III. Title.

CURR QE40 .B35 2001
372.3'57--dc21

2001027622

Contents

Section 2—Ecology

Section 3—The Weather

Introduction

The recent explosion of children's literature has drastically changed the way many educators now teach. Teachers are electing to leave many of the "basal textbooks" behind and incorporate children's literature into the classroom. Teachers are finding that these books, bursting with photographs and colorful illustrations, capture readers' interest and keep the students involved with the topic longer than traditional textbooks. The books on the market offer something for everyone, matching interests and reading abilities of the students to various books. By using children's books, students can go beyond the basic concepts a textbook presents and delve into the topic.

In addition to nonfiction, many creative fiction books are available that are artistically illustrated and cleverly written. Teachers have discovered that these books are fun to read and, often, they can be tied into a science or social studies topic. Students may find that, while studying insects, they're also reading fiction stories such as "The Very Hungry Caterpillar," who undergoes metamorphosis, or "Two Bad Ants," who are *supposed* to be collecting food for the queen and the colony. The subjects of reading and science begin to overlap, giving students more time to do both. Tie in writing activities, art projects, and hands-on activities involving insects, and the concept of "unit studies" comes alive. A unit study incorporates skills and information from several subjects and connects them in a meaningful, stimulating way.

Earth Sciences: Curriculum Resources and Activities for School Librarians and Teachers was created to provide educators with the resources they need to prepare interesting and informative science unit studies quickly and easily. Each chapter provides resources for creating a thematic unit on one specific topic. Using *Curriculum Resources* to plan a unit, teachers can easily pick and choose books and activities to match students' interests and academic abilities. Teaching multilevel classes will no longer be intimidating, and planning time will be dramatically decreased. Teachers who make use of all of the units included in *Curriculum Resources* will cover all the material contained in a standard textbook series, and much more.

Included in this book are the resources needed to prepare stimulating science units for grades K–8. Each topic includes:

1. Key Concepts (Objectives)

   A teacher must have specific goals in mind to plan appropriate activities and lessons. Each major part of *Curriculum Resources* contains a "Key Concepts" section that outlines learning objectives by age level. These "Key Concepts" were derived from studying scope and sequence statements for several school districts, examining textbooks and other printed material, and reviewing standardized tests.

   Through the use of these "Key Concepts," the teacher maintains the flexibility of determining what will be taught and how in-depth the lessons will be. These concepts serve as a guide for lesson planning.

2. Comprehensive Teaching Resources

   Books in the "Comprehensive Teaching Resources" section are in-depth resources that cover more than one unit topic. One of these books can serve as a reference guide for your unit and be used to investigate information related to the topic but not specifically covered in that topic.

3. Teaching Resources (Nonfiction Children's Literature)

In the individual subject chapters, books summarized in this subsection are written for children using text they can understand and incorporate illustrations that capture children's interest. These books can be used in place of textbooks to teach the science topic in a more stimulating manner.

Each book is designated "P" for Primary (K–2), "I" for Intermediate (3–5), or "U" for Upper (6–8) grades. These designations indicate what age level each book's text is geared toward. Each teacher can then decide how best to use a specific book in overall lesson planning. Not all books will be needed to teach the basic concepts of a topic, but the variety of books listed will give teachers the opportunity to choose books that complement their own teaching style.

4. Reading Selections (Fiction Children's Literature)

Each subject chapter includes summaries of a variety of fiction books. These books build on the science topic through engaging stories and enjoyable illustrations. Select a variety of fiction books at various reading levels for independent reading and for shared reading times as well. Not only will these fiction books reinforce reading skills, they can also be used to reinforce the science goals and the vocabulary associated with them.

5. Science Activities

A key segment of any unit study is hands-on experimenting by the student. It is important to supplement teaching resources with projects and experiments from the "Science Activities" subsection of each subject chapter. Ideas are presented for projects that actively involve the students and expand on the science topic. Choose activities that employ a variety of skills—such as research, prediction, and comparison—and incorporate other subjects such as mathematics and English.

Rather than providing page after page of worksheets, enrichment and enhancing activities challenge students to think more creatively and in-depth about the topic. The large variety of activities offered allows the teacher to choose those that most closely match the interests and needs of the students.

Most of the activities listed require the use of everyday household items. This keeps preparation time simple and costs low. Also, activities can be easily modified to different ability levels. Incorporating a few of these activities into the teaching of a subject will increase the interest level of the student and make the lesson more fun for teacher and student alike.

6. Creative Writing and Art Activities

Immediately following the science activities are subsections that expand the science topic into other subject areas. Activities are provided in the areas of reading, writing, and art. Some activities correspond to a fiction book listed in the "Reading Selections" subsection of the chapter and relate the activity to the story. Other activities stand alone and can be assigned with no prior reading required. Again, these activities can be easily modified to various ability levels and encourage creative expression and reasoning skills.

7. Additional Resources

The "Additional Resources" section at the end of each major part lists experiment books, addresses of agencies and related organizations, names of magazines, and Web sites that will provide teachers with more information on the unit topic. The experiment books are available from the library and provide ideas for additional experiments. With all of these resources at their fingertips, teachers should never run out of ideas.

Curriculum Resources places a variety of resources at your fingertips to plan lessons for an entire unit. If you are a person who likes to be very structured, you can write an outline for each unit, with daily lessons. If you are a flexible, go-with-the-flow type of person, you can simply pick and choose from the resources and activities as your day develops. With the variety of books and activities included, you can quickly select an activity that will engage your class for 5 minutes or 45 minutes, based on your needs.

Using *Curriculum Resources*, the process of selecting activities and resources and planning your unit can be accomplished in less than an hour. The result can be three weeks or more of lessons. After planning several units, this process will become second nature and take even less time. With unit studies, lesson planning becomes easier and teaching becomes more fun. Watch the enthusiasm for science in your classroom grow, and revive the joy of learning.

Experiments and the Scientific Method

An important part of science education is teaching children how to think "scientifically" and develop problem-solving skills. This can be done effectively through hands-on demonstrations, activities, and experiments. The "Experiment Books" subsection in the "Additional Resources" section in each major part lists books that are filled with experiments relating to the topic. In addition to these books, some books (noted with a "+") in the "Teaching Resources" subsection in each chapter also contain experiments.

Science education would be incomplete without studying different methods researchers use to make discoveries and develop new theories. Students should learn how to apply the scientific method by doing experiments themselves. Understanding this process will strengthen problem-solving skills.

Scientific research can involve a variety of techniques. Some of the methods scientists use are:

1. *Observing nature*: Learning about the life cycle of a butterfly or how average temperatures determine when crops should be planted are examples of how observing nature provides information that can be used in other areas of study.

2. *Classifying data*: By comparing and contrasting characteristics of different objects or animals, relationships can be determined.

3. *Using logic*: When a specific principle is demonstrated repeatedly, it may logically become a scientific principle of law. For example, objects with less density than water will float. Obviously, not every object in existence was tested before this principle was formed.

4. *Conducting experiments*: This is the major process for developing and proving theories.

5. *Forming a hypothesis*: Scientists may try to explain information received by creating a theory. For example, astronomers found that Uranus was not always in the position they calculated it should be. They then hypothesized the existence of another planet, and later discovered Neptune.

6. *Expressing findings mathematically*: Scientists often explain observations through the use of mathematics. For example, scientists may observe a gravitational relationship between two planets and derive a mathematical equation expressing that relationship. This equation can then be used to predict the gravitational relationship between other planets.

7. *Pure accident*: There is always the unique case of "stumbling onto a discovery." The discovery of penicillin is an excellent example.

When performing a science experiment or project, students should strive to follow a logical, scientific method, such as the following format:

1. *Identify the problem*: What does the student want to find out or expect to learn?

2. *Develop a hypothesis*: What does the student predict will happen?

3. *Describe the procedure and materials*: What steps will be taken to try to solve the problem? What materials will be used?

4. *Record observations/data*: What happened? What results were obtained? When appropriate, data should be recorded in graph form to make it easier to determine patterns and relationships.

5. *Generate conclusions*: What can be learned from the observations made? What conclusions can be made from the data collected?

By following this scientific method, students should learn problem-solving skills and be able to identify a problem and determine possible methods to solve it. The more frequently the students perform experiments, the more familiar they will become with the scientific method. For this reason, educators should strive to include as many hands-on activities as possible in their lesson plans.

Problem-solving skills can be used in many activities included in the subject chapters. Strengthening life-long skills such as problem solving will benefit any student.

THE EARTH

- Key Concepts

- Comprehensive Teaching Resources

- Chapter 1: Rocks, Minerals, and Soil

- Chapter 2: Bodies of Water

- Chapter 3: Oceans

- Chapter 4: Landforms and Geological Processes

- Additional Resources

Key Concepts

■ Primary Concepts

Students will be able to:

1. Compare, contrast, and classify various rocks according to color, size, and shape (Chapter 1).

2. Locate (on a model) and name the three basic layers of the Earth (inner and outer core, mantle, crust) (Chapter 1).

3. Understand that most of the Earth is covered with water (Chapters 2, 3).

4. Recognize that fresh water (lakes, ponds, and rivers) is different from salty ocean water (Chapters 2, 3).

5. Identify the bodies of water on Earth (oceans, lakes, rivers, ponds) (Chapters 2, 3).

6. Recognize and compare the various landforms: valleys, mountains, plains, and hills (Chapter 4).

7. Understand that the Earth is affected and changed by environmental factors (erosion, floods, volcanoes, etc.) (Chapters 1, 4).

■ Intermediate Concepts

Students will be able to:

1. Name and describe the three layers of the Earth (inner and outer core, mantle, crust) (Chapter 1).

2. Identify and describe the layers in soil (topsoil, subsoil) (Chapter 1).

3. Identify the agents of erosion and explain the process involved in each (Chapter 1).

4. Cite examples of common minerals found in the Earth's crust and name some of their attributes (Chapter 1).

5. Explain how igneous, metamorphic, and sedimentary rocks are formed and classify samples of each (Chapter 1).

6. Describe the following natural resources: air, water, soil, fuels, metals, and gems (Chapters 1, 2).

7. Differentiate between physical and chemical weathering, citing causes and examples of each (Chapters 1, 4).

8. Explain factors that change the Earth's crust (e.g., water, wind, volcanoes, earthquakes, and living things) and understand the terms *erosion* and *weathering* (Chapter 4).

9. Identify different formations within caves and how they develop (stalactites, stalagmites) (Chapter 4).

3

■ Upper Concepts

Students will be able to:

1. Explain how the relative age of rocks is scientifically determined (Chapter 1).

2. Explain the method of radiometric dating and the theory behind its use (Chapter 1).

3. Differentiate between the life forms believed to have existed in the Paleozoic, Mesozoic, and Cenozoic eras (Chapter 1).

4. Diagram the water cycle (Chapter 2).

5. Explain groundwater and describe its effects on various land zones (Chapter 2).

6. Describe the effects that groundwater has on subterranean features (Chapter 2).

7. Name and locate the major U.S. river systems (Chapter 2).

8. Explain how lakes and ponds are formed (Chapter 2).

9. Name and locate the major U.S. lakes (Chapter 2).

10. Identify the four major oceans and locate them on a map (Chapter 3).

11. Identify the depths and sizes of these oceans (Chapter 3).

12. Research and locate the deepest ocean trenches (Chapter 3).

13. Understand that over 70 percent of the Earth's surface is covered by water (Chapter 3).

14. Discuss minerals recovered from the ocean floor (Chapter 3).

15. Define the terms *salinity* and *desalination* (Chapter 3).

16. Explain the occurrence of tides (Chapter 3).

17. Identify and locate the five major oceanic currents on a world map (Chapter 3).

18. Discuss the effects that ocean currents have on the environment (Chapter 3).

19. Discuss the causes of waves (Chapter 3).

20. Locate the following formations on a cross-section drawing of the ocean floor:

continental shelf	abyssal plain
continental slope	seamounts
trenches	guyots

21. Identify and explain how the following are formed (Chapter 3):

baymouth bars	spits
sand bars	sea stacks
coral reefs	sea arches
beaches	sea lanes
longshores	currents

22. Name and label 15 seas, including (Chapter 3):

    Arabian

    Baltic

    Bering

    Black

    Caribbean

Caspian

Corkebass

Mediterranean

North

Red

23. Distinguish between an ocean and a sea (Chapter 3).

24. Consider early oceanographic contributions and their effects on future studies (Chapter 3).

25. Discuss ways in which the study of oceanography will affect the future of humanity (Chapter 3).

26. Describe the theory of plate tectonics (Chapter 4).

27. Differentiate between the plate tectonics theory and the continental drift theory (Chapter 4).

28. Define earthquakes and describe what causes them (Chapter 4).

29. Describe volcanoes, what causes them, and how and where they form (Chapter 4).

30. Do the following in relation to volcanoes (Chapter 4):

Explain what they are.

Identify the locations of volcanoes.

Describe three ways in which volcanoes are formed.

Compare and contrast two kinds of magma that occur in a volcano.

Name four types of volcanic eruptions.

List three types of materials released during these eruptions.

Describe three kinds of volcanic cones.

31. Explain how fissures add substances to the Earth's surface (Chapter 4).

32. Explain the process that occurs in the formation of caves (Chapter 4).

33. Describe Wegener's theory of continental drift. Include the following information (Chapter 4):

Provide a drawing of the supposed supercontinent, Pangaea, and its subsequent breaking apart into the land masses, Laurasia and Condioanaland

Compare these drawings to the present-day continents

List four pieces of evidence that Wegener cited to support his theory

List reasons why his theory was not accepted

34. Do the following in relation to earthquakes (Chapter 4):

Explain what they are.

Demonstrate the relationship between earthquakes and plate boundaries.

Discuss how earthquakes can also take place away from plate boundaries.

Define the terms *focus* and *epicenter*.

Explain what causes seismic waves.

List and describe different types of seismic waves.

Define and discuss the Richter scale.

Describe a natural disaster that was a result of an earthquake.

Name three ways presently used by scientists to predict earthquakes.

35. Define three types of plate boundaries (divergent, convergent, transform) (Chapter 4).

36. List two features that may form as plates collide (volcanoes, mountains) (Chapter 4).

37. Map the location of the Earth's mountain ranges (Chapter 4).

38. Name the four main types of mountains and how they are formed (fault block, dome, fold, volcanic) (Chapter 4).

39. Explain how islands are formed and locate the following major islands on a map (Chapter 4):

Greenland	Falkland Islands
Iceland	Sicily
Hawaii	Madagascar
Cuba	Borneo
Virgin Islands	New Zealand

Comprehensive Teaching Resources

The following table lists books that cover a wide range of topics about the Earth. One of these books could serve as your main teaching guide while studying this unit. Each book is listed with a short summary, and the chapters in this book that it applies to are noted. The books are listed by degree of difficulty, easiest to most difficult.

BOOK AND SUMMARY	AUTHOR	CHAPTERS			
		1	2	3	4
Our Planet Earth (Random House, 1993) Brief, easy-to-read text introduces geology, geography, and natural resources of the world.	Keith Lye	X	X	X	X
Forces of Nature (Western, 1991) Covers landforms, rocks, minerals, and other subjects in brief text and good illustrations.	Anita Ganeri	X	X		X
Earth (Dorling Kindersley, 1993) Brief text and wonderful pictures introduce the Earth's crust, landforms, volcanoes, rocks and minerals, erosion, rivers, and oceans.	Eyewitness Visual Dictionary	X	X	X	X
Earth: All About Earthquakes, Volcanoes, Glaciers, Oceans, and More (Greey dePencier Books, 1989) Easy-to-understand text and bright illustrations cover earthquakes, volcanoes, glaciers, and oceans.	Carol Allen			X	X
The Random House Book of 1001 Questions & Answers About Planet Earth (Random House, 1993) Question-and-answer format covers topics such as physical features, volcanoes, earthquakes, oceans, and resources.	Brian Williams and Brenda Williams	X	X	X	X
The Usborne Book of the Earth (Usborne Publishing, 1993) Contains information on rivers, rocks and minerals, volcanoes, oceans, and the Earth's structure.	Fiona Watt	X	X	X	X
Eyewitness Visual Dictionary (Dorling Kindersley, 1992) Excellent resource with brief text and great pictures. Includes sections on Earth's crust, mountains, volcanoes, rocks and minerals, fossils, erosion, caves, glaciers, and rivers/oceans.	Dorling Kindersley	X	X	X	X
The Young Naturalist (EDC Publishing, 1991) Comprehensive introduction to ponds, rivers, and oceans. Contains many ideas for collecting, observing, and experimenting with the world around us.	Andrew Mitchell		X	X	

Each chapter in this section lists reference books that focus on the specific area of the Earth being addressed. These books can be used to complement and expand upon the basic information provided in the comprehensive resource books listed in the previous table.

The reference books in each chapter have been classified by age level to help you select those that best fit the needs and interests of your student(s).

Chapter 1
Rocks, Minerals, and Soil

■ Teaching Resources

Books containing experiment(s) relating to the subject matter are marked with a plus sign (+) before and after the title.

P *Fossils Tell of Long Ago,* by Aliki (Thomas Y. Crowell, 1972)
Appealing illustrations with simple text explain what fossils are, how they were formed, and what they tell us about long ago.

P *From Sea to Salt,* by Ali Mitgutsch (Carolrhoda Books, 1985)
Simple illustrations and text describe salt extraction from mines and the sea.

P *From Swamp to Coal,* by Ali Mitgutsch (Carolrhoda Books, 1985)
Simple illustrations and text explain coal formation and mining.

P *How to Dig a Hole to the Other Side of the World,* by Faith McNulty (Harper & Row, 1979)
Follows a child on an imaginary 8,000-mile trip through the Earth.

P *Rock Collecting,* by Roma Gans (Thomas Y. Crowell, 1984)
Simplistic text that includes descriptions of the three types of rocks.

P *Rocks and Minerals, a New True Book,* by Illa Podendorf (Children's Press, 1982)
Easy-to-read form, with photographs, describes rocks and minerals throughout the world.

P/I *One Small Square Backyard,* by Donald M. Silver (W. H. Freeman, 1993)
Cutaway illustrations and helpful text take a closer look at the Earth's ecosystem.

P/I +*Rocks and Minerals,*+ by Steve Parker (Dorling Kindersley, 1993)
Brief text with nice illustrations in handheld size. Describes different types of rocks and minerals, erosion, locations, and gems, and includes numerous activities.

P/I/U *Crystal and Gem,* by Dr. R. F. Symes and Dr. R. R. Harding (Alfred A. Knopf, 1991)
A great resource for exploring all types of crystals and gems.

P/I/U *Fossils,* by Paul D. Taylor, Ph.D. (Alfred A. Knopf, 1990)
Covers many different types of fossils with beautiful pictures and concise text.

P/I/U *Rocks and Minerals,* by Dr. R. F. Symes (Alfred A. Knopf, 1988)
Excellent resource for all levels covering the creation, erosion, mining, and uses of rocks and minerals.

I   *Rocks and Minerals,* by Herbert S. Zim (Econo-Clad, 1999)
A good resource for information on rocks and minerals.

I/U +*Crystals and Crystal Gardens You Can Grow,*+ by Jean Stangl (Franklin Watts, 1990)
Scientific explanations of crystal formations, tips for growing them, and experiments to grow your own.

I/U *Fossils,* by Frank H. T. Rhodes, Herbert S. Zim, and Paul R. Shaffer (Golden Books Publishing, 2000)
More than 400 color illustrations make this a great resource book about fossil formation and identification.

I/U *Sand Dunes,* by Jan Gumprecht Bannan (Carolrhoda Books, 1989)
The book focuses on the dune areas in Oregon and is an excellent source for explaining sand formations and the forces that shape them.

U   *Fossils,* by Roy A. Gallant (Franklin Watts, 1985)
Good paleontology resource describing fossilization, evolution, and what fossils can tell us.

■ Reading Selections

Books marked with an asterisk (*) before and after the title are related to activities in the activity sections of this chapter.

The Adventures of King Midas, by Lynne Reid Banks (Camelot, 1993)
> King Midas regrets his wish that everything he touches should turn to gold and faces many tests to try to undo it. (Chapter Book)

Anansi and the Moss-Covered Rock, by Eric Kimmel (Holiday House, 1990)
> Anansi, the spider, uses a strange moss-covered rock in the forest to trick all the other animals, until Little Bush Deer decides to teach Anansi a lesson.

The Bite of the Gold Bug, by Barthe DeClements (Puffin, 1994)
> A boy and his father overcome many challenges while prospecting for gold in Alaska in 1898.

Chang's Paper Pony, by Eleanor Coerr (Harper Trophy, 1993)
> Chang, who lives in San Francisco during the gold rush, longs for a pony his family cannot afford.

The Country Bunny and the Little Gold Shoes, by Dubose Heyward (Houghton Mifflin, 1974)
> A country bunny attains the position of Easter Bunny despite the fact that she is the mother of 21 children.

Fat Chance, Claude, by Joan Lowery Nixon (Viking Kestrel, 1987)
> Shirley and Claude grow up and meet in the gold-mining hills in Colorado.

From Afar It Is an Island, by Bruno Munari (World Publishers), 1972
> Text and illustrations of many different stones and pictures that can be painted on them.

The Hill and the Rock, by David McKee (Anderson Press, 1999)
> After the Quests move the rock that blocks the view from their house on top of the hill, the hill deflates, and they find themselves living in a valley instead of on a hill.

Huan Ching and the Golden Fish, by Michael Reeser (Raintree, 1989)
> Huan Ching makes a kite shaped like a goldfish to fly in the contest on the Chinese kite flying holiday.

If You Are a Hunter of Fossils, by Byrd Baylor (Aladdin Paperbacks, 1984)
> A fossil hunter describes how the Earth may have appeared in prehistoric times.

Jeremy Visick, by David Wiseman (Houghton Mifflin, 1990)
> Matthew is drawn to help a boy lost in a mining accident a century before. (Chapter Book)

The King's Fifth, by Scott O'Dell (Houghton Mifflin, 1976)
> Esteban is on trial for withholding from the King the gold he has found. While awaiting trial, Esteban reminisces about the adventures he had with a band of conquistadors. (Chapter Book)

The Magic School Bus Inside the Earth, by Joanna Cole (Scholastic, 1989)
> Ms. Frizzle takes her class on a special field trip to learn about rocks and the formation of the Earth.

The Night Flight, by Joanne Ryder (Econo-Clad, 1999)
> Anna is taken to a secret waterfall by a stone lion who comes alive in the park after dark.

Stone Soup, by Tony Ross (Dial Books for Young Readers, 1992)
> Mother Hen keeps the Big Bad Wolf from eating her by making him a pot of her grandmother's famous stone soup.

Sylvester and the Magic Pebble, by William Steig (Econo-Clad, 1999)
> A donkey with a magic pebble asks it to turn him into a rock and then cannot hold the pebble to turn back to normal.

Words of Stone, by Kevin Henkes (Puffin, 1993)
> Blaze's world is changed forever after meeting Joselle, who helps him deal with his fears and feelings of loss. (Chapter Book)

The Wretched Stone, by Chris Vans Allsburg (Houghton Mifflin, 1991)
> A glowing stone has a transforming effect on the crew of a ship.

Zekmet, the Stone Carver, by Mary Stolz (Harcourt Brace Jovanovich, 1988)
> A tale of a stonecutter who designs and begins work on the Egyptian sphinx.

The following books are out of print, but may be available at the local library.

Angelina's Birthday Surprise, by Katharine Holabird (Potter, 1989)
> Angelina loves to race her bicycle, until she crashes into a rock.

Chocolate Mud Cake, by Harriet Ziefert (Harper & Row, 1988)
> Two girls have fun creating a chocolate cake out of dirt, sand, and stones, but quickly abandon their masterpiece for a real snack.

Deep Down Underground, by Olivier Dunrea (Macmillan, 1989)
> A number book presented by animals burrowing deep underground.

Fire and Stone, by Ursula K. Le Guin (Atheneum, 1989)
> Min and Podo help stop the fire-breathing dragon by feeding him stones.

The Fish of Gold, by The Brothers Grimm, adapted by M. Eulalia Valeri (Silver Burdett, 1985)
> A poor fisherman catches a fish of gold that promises to grant any wish the fisherman may have if he will set the fish free.

McGoogan Moves the Mighty Rock, by Dick Gackenbach (Harper & Row, 1981)
> McGoogan helps a rock that desperately wishes to see the sea.

The Rock, by Peter Parnall (Collier Macmillan, 1991)
> As years pass, a rock provides shelter, food, and a resting place for people and animals.

Rocks in My Pocket, by Marc Harshman (Cobblehill Books, 1991)
> A family in the mountains uses rocks they find around their farm for all sorts of useful purposes.

*Solomon's Secret,** by Saviour Pirotta (Dial Books for Young Readers, 1989)
> Solomon visits his neighbors who have a wonderful copper kettle that allows Solomon to travel the world without leaving their backyard.

*The Town That Moved,** by Mary Jane Finsand (Carolrhoda Books, 1983)
> When iron ore is discovered under a Minnesota town, the people decide to move the town rather than have it destroyed.

■ Science Activities

Soil Comparisons

Ask the students to bring in five soil samples from different areas (by a river, in a garden, in a forest, on a hillside, etc.). Do the following demonstration in class: Place one cup of soil from each area in a separate 1-pint jar. Add water until the water level is 1 inch below the top of the jar. Stir, then let it settle. Compare the amount of clay, silt, fine sand, and coarse sand in each sample. As a math exercise, students can graph the results of each sample. Students can also determine the percentages of each type of product in comparison to the whole.

How Soil Is Made

Demonstrate how soil is made by doing the following experiments with the students:

- Rub two pieces of limestone, bricks, or concrete together. After a while, you can see a few fine particles collect.
- Heat a small piece of limestone over a flame or hotplate. Drop it quickly into a pan of ice water. The rock will break or crack as it contracts.
- Fill an old glass container (that has a lid) with water. Screw the lid on tightly and put the jar where it will freeze. Note what happens to the jar. (The jar will crack, or possibly break. If using your freezer for this experiment, you may want to place the jar inside a plastic bag to catch any debris.)

Ask the students how these events occur on Earth to cause the formation of soil. (Number 1 represents glaciers grinding rocks together. Number 2 represents the sun heating rocks and the night air cooling them. Number 3 demonstrates how forceful water can be when it enters cracks in rocks and then freezes.)

What Is Soil Made Of?

- Have one student fill a glass jar halfway with water, then put a handful of soil in it. Ask another student to stir the mixture with a stick to combine the soil with the water. Then watch the soil settle into different layers. Ask the class: What settles to the bottom first? What settles above that? What settles into the top layer?

• Even if you wait a long time, the water won't become completely clear. Small pieces of clay and bits of leaves and plants will remain floating on the surface. Try this experiment using soil from different places: a garden, a forest, a farm, and so forth. Ask the students if they think the different layers will always be the same thickness.

How Much Air Is in the Soil?

Do the following experiment to demonstrate to the class that there is air in the soil.

• Fill a small tin can with water and pour the water into a measuring cup. Note the exact amount of water you have.

• Fill this same can with garden soil. Push the soil into the can so it is tightly compacted. You have now filled the same amount of space with soil as you did with water. (You have the same volume of soil as water.)

• Pour the soil into the water and stir it. Measure the mixture. Ask the students: Does it fill twice as much space? (Why not?)

• See if your students can determine how much air was in the can of soil. Try this experiment with different types of soil and ask the students to note whether all soil contains the same amount of air.

Soil Content

• Ask your students to collect lumps of soil from a field that has been heavily farmed and an undisturbed area such as a forest or along a fencerow and bring the soil to class.

• Have one student measure 2 cups of soil from one of the samples and place it in a strainer. Ask another student to suspend the strainer over a bowl and add 1 pint of water. Wait for two minutes.

• After the time is up, have a third student measure how much water has drained off the soil. Repeat this process with the second soil sample and other students. Ask the class: Is there a difference in the amount of water that has run off each soil sample? If so, why? (The amount of organic matter present in the soil will affect the amount of water that runs off.) What does this experiment demonstrate about erosion?

Soil Samples

• Ask your students to collect large soil samples (measuring approximately 1 foot square and 2 or 3 inches deep) and place the samples in separate brown grocery bags. They should collect samples from as many of the following places as possible: below the leaves in a forest, a field that has been heavily farmed, a fencerow, a riverbank, and an eroded hillside. Have them bring the samples to class.

• In class, lay out pieces of newspaper and spread out one of the samples on them. Ask the students to examine the soil carefully, looking for small living things. (They should collect these specimens in separate jars.) Have a student list the animals found in each sample of soil and how many of each there are. Some of the creatures you could see are worms, grubs, snails, slugs, insects, and spiders.

• Ask the class: Which sample has the most animal life? Does the amount of animal life appear to have any correlation to the looseness or texture of the soil?

• You can also strengthen math skills by having the students calculate how many animals would be in 1 square yard, 20 square feet, 1 acre, and so forth. Or students can graph the results of the different types of soil.

Soil Protection

- Obtain two heavy cardboard boxes (available at shipping stores or your local supermarket). The boxes should be approximately 16 by 12 by 4 inches. Remove the lids and cut a "V" shape out of one of the ends of each box. Cover the inside of the box with a plastic trash bag.
- Ask a student to fill both boxes with soil (the same kind). In one box, top the soil with mulch. Set the boxes on a table, propping up the uncut end of the boxes so that the boxes are sloping (V-side down). Have another student place two chairs or stools next to the table (and under the boxes) and put a bowl on each of them. (The bowls will be used to catch any water runoff from the boxes of soil.)
- Using the same amount of water, and pouring it at the same rate from the same height, pour water onto each soil sample. Observe how fast the water drains off each sample. Have a third student measure how much water is collected from each sample.
- Repeat this activity using a piece of sod that is the size of the box (grass and all) and the soil sample you used above that did not have the mulch on it. Ask the class if they can explain how the grass protects the soil.

Minerals

Have the students search their houses for some common uses of minerals. They should look at household products such as talcum powder, table salt, epsom salt, baking soda, baking powder, milk of magnesia, and sandpaper. Ask the students: Do these products contain minerals? If so, which ones? How is each mineral used? How many other uses of minerals can you name? Upper-level students can discuss the difference between minerals, rocks, salts, elements, and compounds. (Minerals are considered to be ores found in nature.)

Human Requirements

Have the class research what minerals the human body requires to grow and function, then make a list of these minerals and find out what the USDA's minimum daily requirements are for each. As a group, plan a menu for one day that would meet all of the USDA's minimum requirements.

Famous Rock Formations

Have students look on a map and locate some famous rocks, such as

the Rock of Gibraltar

Plymouth Rock

Ayers Rock

the Rosetta Stone

Diamond Head

Then have them check an encyclopedia to see if they can identify any other famous rocks or stones. They should locate those also.

Rocks and Energy

Ask students to answer the following questions or do the research to find out how rocks can give us energy:

- Rocks can store solar energy during the day or collect heat from a fire. How would this information be useful?

- Research some of the cooking techniques of Polynesians who built fires on rocks and then used the rocks for their cooking. (This is the basic principle behind clambakes, as well.) Try cooking with rocks by setting up a similar situation in an outdoor grill. (Adult supervision is required!)
- Coal is a rock that can be burned to release energy. What is coal made of? Make a chart explaining and showing how coal is formed.
- What are the different types of coal (anthracite, bituminous, sub-bituminous)? Which U.S. states have large deposits of each type of coal? On a map of the United States, indicate where different types of coal are found.
- There are other types of fuel that are similar to coal but contain a higher percentage of water, such as brown coal, lignite, and peat. Research these resources. Are any of these used as a main source of heat in the world today? Are any used for other energy purposes?

Comparing Rocks

- There are three major types of rocks: igneous, sedimentary, and metamorphic. Make sure that the students understand the difference between these three groups.
- Ask the students where they think most igneous rocks are found. Make a class chart divided into three sections for the different types of rocks. Using the students' answers, list examples of each type of rock and where they are usually found.
- Ask the students to collect different types of rocks and bring them to class. Carefully tap the different rocks with a hammer. Ask the students to explain why some break into small pieces, others just chip, and still others remain in one piece. Can they classify these rocks as igneous, sedimentary, and metamorphic?
- Add a few drops of vinegar to some of the rocks. Some may bubble when the vinegar is added. These rocks have carbonates in them. Using the results of the vinegar test, chart which rocks are carbonates and which are silicates.

Coal Products

Discuss what products we get from coal. Have students research coal and find five examples of coal products that fall into each of these categories: coke, coal tar, light oil, ammonia, and coal gas.

Coal Mining

Have students research the following questions: What are the different ways in which coal is mined? What dangers are associated with coal mining? What controversies surround the mining of coal in the United States? Have students design a safety poster warning miners about some of the dangers associated with their profession.

Math Games

- Play or Pass (for two to four players)

    You will need 12 smooth rocks and a can or box. On nine of the rocks, paint (with nail polish or a permanent marker) the numbers 1 through 9 (one number on each rock). On the remaining three rocks, paint an "X."

As each person takes a turn, he or she should decide to "play" or "pass." If the person "plays," that person picks a rock out of the can (without looking at it). If the rock has a number on it, the player keeps it. If the rock has an "X" on it, the player returns it to the can along with one of the numbered rocks he or she has already picked.

The game ends when a round occurs in which all players have passed. The winner is the player whose rocks, when added together, total the highest number.

You can develop variations on this game by adding more rocks and numbers to the game or by using slightly larger rocks and painting simple equations on them. The students must solve the equation to keep the rock and determine their score at the end of the game.

- Rock, Scissors, Paper (two players)

    This game is played with three hand shapes: a fist for a rock, two fingers in a V-shape to imitate scissors, and an open hand for paper.

    Players hide their hands behind their backs. At the count of three, both players put out one hand, making one of the above signs.

    If both players make the same sign, there is no score.

    If the signs are different, a point is awarded as follows: rock beats scissors (rocks can break scissors); scissors beats paper (scissors can cut paper); paper beats rock (paper can cover a rock).

    Choose a winning score at the beginning of the game, and play until one of the contestants achieves that score.

A Magical Crystal Garden

- Demonstrate how crystals form on rocks in a class crystal garden. You'll need several rocks, 1/4 cup of water, 2 tablespoons of salt, blue food coloring, and a pie plate.
- Arrange the rocks in the pie plate.
- Heat the water and mix the salt with the water until it completely dissolves. Add two or three drops of the food coloring to the water. Stir. Pour the solution over the rocks in the pie plate.
- Put your rock garden in the sun and wait until all of the water evaporates. Blue crystals will be left on the rocks. Ask the students if they can explain why. (Salt is a crystal. It returns to its natural form when the water evaporates. The more water that evaporates, the more crystals are formed on top of each other.)
- Try this experiment in a shady area where the water would evaporate more slowly. The crystals would be larger. Vary the amount of saltwater and food coloring used and see what the results are.

Another Crystal Garden

Another way to create crystals is by replacing the rocks in the previous experiment with charcoal briquettes, as follows:

- Sprinkle a few drops of food coloring over the briquettes.
- Mix 3 tablespoons each of salt, liquid bluing, and clear ammonia in a paper cup and pour the solution over the charcoal. (BE CAREFUL: Don't smell the ammonia directly!)
- Your crystals will begin to grow in just a few hours. You can repeat this process each day to keep your crystals growing.

Make Your Own Crystals

- Heat a pan of water until it is warm. Stir in alum until no more will dissolve. Cool. When crystals form, remove some of the biggest ones. Heat the remaining solution again and add more alum until no more will dissolve. Cool. Pour the solution into a tall glass.
- Ask a student to tie one end of a thin string around the largest crystal that you removed from the pan of water and tie the other end to a pencil, then lay the pencil across the top of the glass and lower the crystal into the solution.
- Have another student place the glass in a quiet spot and let it sit for three or four days. Crystals should appear along the string as it is pulled out of the solution.
- You can repeat this experiment using epsom salts, sugar, or table salt.

Weathering

To demonstrate physical weathering and its effect on rocks, try this experiment. You'll need a glass bottle, a cork to fit the top of the bottle, and water. Fill the bottle with water. Put the cork on the top of the bottle and place it in the freezer. After several hours, check the bottle. Is the cork still in place? (Probably not.) Can the students explain why? (Water expands as it freezes, taking up more space in the frozen state. This expansion forces the cork out of the top of the bottle because there isn't enough room for it anymore. If the cork is on too tightly, the bottle will crack, just as a rock cracks when water freezes inside it.)

■ Creative Writing Activities

Following are instructions to give the students for various writing activities.

- Pretend you are a reporter for a newspaper. You have been sent to cover the story of a small town that has discovered it cannot remain in its present location and has decided to undertake the task of moving every building in the town to a new location. What angle would you use to cover this story? You could interview residents to get their reactions before, during, and after the job is done. Also, do a follow-up story one year after the move to see how the town is doing in its new location. (*The Town That Moved* by Finsand)
- Pretend you have just discovered gold in a creek that runs behind your house. How would you feel? What would you do with your newfound wealth? Write an article for a magazine describing your find and what you plan to do with it.
- Discuss the story of King Midas (the king who was granted his wish that everything he touched would turn to gold). Would you like to be in that situation? Write a story about a wish that you made that was granted. Were the results what you expected? Were you happy with what you wished for?
- Look up the definition of the word *cornerstone*. Discuss its meaning and importance. Write an essay about a person you know who can be considered the "cornerstone" of your life. Be sure to give specific reasons for your choice.
- It is often said, "Every cloud has a silver lining." What is the meaning of this phrase? Write a story that demonstrates this saying. You can also make a cloud with a silver lining by drawing a cloud on white paper and cutting it out. Then draw the same cloud, only slightly larger, on a piece of cardboard. Cut it out and cover the cardboard with aluminum foil. Glue the white cloud in the center of the silver cloud so that the edges of the silver cloud show around the white one. You could even write your story on the white cloud.
- If you had a magic pebble that would grant any wish, what wish would you make? (*Sylvester and the Magic Pebble* by Steig)

- You found an old, copper kettle at a local flea market and bought it. When you got the pot home, you decided to clean it and use it to make soup in. Whenever you boil water in this copper kettle, a lovely fragrance fills your home and then . . . . Finish this story with your own ending and adventure. (*Solomon's Secret* by Pirotta)

- You have just discovered a new type of rock that is very special. Why is it special, and how can it be used? Will you become famous for your discovery? Write a "news release" describing your discovery and the experiments you performed on it that prove its worth.

- What is fool's gold? How did it get its name? Write a story about someone who thinks he or she has struck it rich. How would this change that person's life? What happens when the person finds out he or she really isn't rich after all?

- Compare several different versions of the Grimm Brothers' tale of a magical fish who grants wishes to a poor fisherman. How are the fish characters in the different stories similar? How do they differ? How do the wishes of the different "fishermen" compare? What other similarities and differences can you find? (*The Fish of Gold* adapted by Valeri; *The Magic Fish* by Littledale)

- Have you ever been discouraged when you had difficulty learning how to do something? Write a letter of encouragement to someone you know who could use a "pep talk." (If you can't think of anyone in particular, write your letter to the character Angelina in *Angelina's Birthday Surprise* by Holabird.)

- What would it be like to live underground? Write a science fiction story that describes your life in an underground world. Be sure to include detailed descriptions of what your world looks like. (*Deep Down Underground* by Dunrea)

- Pretend you are mining gold during the Gold Rush of 1849 in California. Write a journal that tells about your daily activities and what life in general is like in the mining towns of this era.

- "It was a dark and stormy night. The rain was pounding the windshield of our station wagon so hard, we could barely see where we were going. The road was made of dirt and was quickly turning to mud. Suddenly, the wheels of the car got stuck in the muddy road. Now what would we do?" Continue this story, explaining where you are, why you are there, and what happens to you.

■ Art Activities

Following are instructions to give the students for various art activities.

- What animals make their homes underground? Choose an animal that lives underground and sketch a scene that shows this animal's underground home.

- Make a diorama of *The Magic School Bus Inside the Earth* by Cole, using the following instructions:

    Cut a peephole in one of the short ends of a shoe box. Cut out the entire other short end of the box and cover it with colored plastic wrap. This allows light into your scene and makes it easier to view.

    Remove the lid of the shoebox and create your scene inside so that it faces the peephole. Draw a school bus with you at a window of it or cut a picture of a school bus out of a magazine and glue on a picture of yourself at the window. Glue real rocks to the bottom of the box or make rocks by painting crumpled-up newspaper. Be creative! You can paint the insides of the box or even suspend things from the inside of the lid.

    When you are finished, replace the box's lid and view your scene through the peephole.

- Gather rocks from your yard, the park, or around the neighborhood. Wash the rocks and then, with tempera paint or finger paint, paint the rocks to look like animals, faces, or different foods, or just paint them with your favorite colors and designs. These can make lovely gifts for friends, or you can start your own collection.

- Find the perfect rock to have as a pet. (Ask one of your parents or grandparents about the "Pet Rock" fad.) Decorate the rock you choose to give it the special features you desire. Make a home for your pet as well. You can build a cage out of Popsicle sticks or toothpicks, or you can build it a little home. You might even sew a special cushion for it to sleep on. Do you know someone who has always wanted a pet but can't have one? Give your pet rock to that person as a gift.

- Design a piece of jewelry using rocks and stones that you find in your neighborhood. Draw the outline of the piece of jewelry you want to make. Glue the rocks and stones you chose in the proper place on your drawing.

- Make a stone sculpture using the instructions that follow:

  Gather rocks of different shapes and colors. Wash the rocks you have chosen to remove any dirt. Let the rocks dry.

  Use your imagination to design your sculpture. You may want to sketch it out on paper while your rocks are drying. You can make a building, a piece of modern art, or the statue of a person or animal. Flat, triangular shapes could be feet, wings, or ears. Round, long shapes could be legs, arms, or tails. Thick, square, or round shapes make good bodies. Small stones can be used for eyes, noses, beaks, or mouths.

- Make your own fossils using the following recipe:

> 1/2 cup corn starch
> 1 cup baking soda
> 5/8 cup (1/2 cup + 2 tablespoons) water
>
> Mix together. Cook over medium heat until thick. Let mixture cool. (Makes four or five fossils.)
> While you wait for the mixture to cool, gather items that would make good fossil impressions (uniquely shaped rocks, small plastic toys, shells, bones, etc.). When the mixture is cool, form it into small balls and flatten it between two pieces of waxed paper. Press one of the items you gathered into the mixture and then remove it.
> Let the flattened ball dry completely, and you have made your own fossil. (*If You Are a Hunter of Fossils* by Baylor)

- Create an aluminum sculpture. Gather different shapes of boxes, paper tubes (e.g., from toilet tissue, paper towels, wrapping paper), straws, cone-shaped drinking cups, and so forth. Wrap the objects you have gathered in aluminum foil and then glue or tape them together to create your own piece of modern (or traditional) sculpture.

- On one side of a piece of paper, draw a picture of the scene that you see outside a window in your home. On the other side of the paper, draw the picture of a scene that you would like to see when you gaze out your window. (*The Hill and the Rock* by McKee)

- Make a tic-tac-toe set out of rocks and Popsicle sticks. Find 10 fairly flat rocks in your yard, neighborhood, or park. Wash and dry the rocks and then paint an "O" on five of the rocks and an "X" on the other five. Glue four Popsicle sticks together so they resemble a "#" symbol to serve as the board for your tic-tac-toe game. When you play, place your rocks on the board just like you would play tic-tac-toe with paper and pencil.

- Make a personalized paperweight. Find a medium-sized rock. Wash the rock and let it dry. Decorate the paperweight to reflect your favorite sport or favorite flower, with the title of a favorite book, or with your name and some special designs. These paperweights can make great presents for friends and family members, too.

- Make a tambourine using pebbles as the shakers, as follows:

     Decorate the bottoms of two paper plates.

     Place the pebbles on the undecorated side of one of the plates.

     Put the second plate on top of the first plate so that the decorated side of each plate is on the outside.

     Staple, or tape, the two plates together around the outside rim. You can also punch holes along the outside rim and sew the plates together with colored string, yarn, or ribbon.

     Staple, or tape, some paper or ribbon streamers to the bottom of your tambourine and start to play!

  You can add to your "rock" band by decorating the outside of an empty (and washed) soda can, placing pebbles inside the can, and taping shut the opening in the top. The noise from shaking the can could be exquisite.
  Or . . . decorate the outside of an empty, washed 2-liter bottle. Place small stones inside the bottle and replace the cap. This sounds more like a muffled drum. You can also use an old plastic container (margarine, oatmeal, shortening can, coffee can, etc.) to get many different effects.

- Using staples or wood glue, fasten pieces of sandpaper to two blocks of wood that will fit easily in the palms of your hands. Rub the two blocks together to make a rough, sandy-sounding melody. You can make other instruments for your band by putting sand or dirt (depending on the sound you want from your instrument) into other containers you have around the house. Also, get a flat piece of board, lay it on the floor, and sprinkle it with sand. Try doing a dance on the sandy surface by shuffling your feet as you dance. This type of dance is known as a "soft shoe."

- Get some dirt from your yard. Place the dirt on a cookie sheet or piece of aluminum foil. Add water to the dirt to make a clay/mud-like substance. See how creative you can get. Make as many different shapes and forms as you can from your dirt.

Chapter 2
Bodies of Water

■ Teaching Resources

Books containing experiment(s) relating to the subject matter are marked with a plus sign (+) before and after the title.

P   The Earth Is Mostly Ocean, by Allan Fowler (Children's Press, 1995)
Introduces the world's oceans and demonstrates how the Earth is covered mostly by ocean water.

P   *Follow the Water from Brook to Ocean,* by Arthur Dorros (Harper Trophy, 1991)
Explains how water journeys from a brook and, eventually, to the ocean.

P   *In the Pond,* by Ermanno Cristini and Luigi Puricelli (Picture Book Studio, 1984)
Wordless book shows the activity of the marshy wetlands.

P   *Seas and Coasts,* by Patience Coster (Children's Press, 1997)
Introduces features of the world's oceans and coastlines, including currents, waves, tides, and sandy and rocky beaches.

P   *Wonders of Rivers,* by Rae Bains (Troll, 1982)
Watercolor illustrations add to the brief text about river formation, origins, and uses.

P/I *All About Ponds,* by Jane Rockwell (Troll, 1984)
Question-and-answer book about pond plants and animals and a pond's life stages.

P/I *Nature Hide and Seek, Rivers and Lakes,* by John Norris Wood (Random House, 1999)
Fold-out pages with hidden animals among water scenes, followed by brief descriptions of the animals found in five different lake and river habitats.

P/I *The River,* by David Bellamy (Crown, 1988)
Story about pond life and the effects of man-made catastrophes on it is told through easy text and watercolor illustrations.

P/I *+River and Oceans,+* by Barbara Taylor (Kingfisher Books, 1993)
Geography facts and experiments to introduce the different forms of water in the world, the water cycle, stages of a river, currents, lakes, and pollution.

P/I *River Life,* by Barbara Taylor (Dorling Kindersley, 1992)
Enlarged pictures and brief text describe animals and plants that live in and along a river.

P/I *Rivers, Ponds and Lakes,* by Anita Ganeri (Dillon, 1992)
Describes how modern life is affecting ponds, rivers, and lakes globally and discusses the possible ways of saving the endangered species in these waterways.

P/I/U *Pond and River,* by Steve Parker (Alfred A. Knopf, 1988)
Details plants and animals found in freshwater.

P/I/U *Pond Life,* by George K. Reid, Ph.D. (Golden Book Publishing, 1990)
Serves as a good pocket reference book when exploring pond life.

I *The Living River,* by Nigel Hester (Franklin Watts, 1991)
Discusses coexistence of fish, plants, insects, and other animals on a river.

I *Oceans,* by Neil Morris (Crabtree, 1995)
Describes the world's five oceans, their movements, effects on the weather, life forms, and the effects of pollution.

I *Oceans,* by Anna O'Mara (Bridgestone Books, 1996)
Gives basic scientific information about the size of the oceans, their floors, mountains, volcanoes, currents, tides, and waves.

I *Oceans,* by Don P. Rothaus (Child's World, 1997)
Describes the characteristics of the oceans, including origins, composition, currents, and effects of the tides.

I *Our Endangered Planet, Groundwater,* by Mary Hoff and Mary M. Rodgers (Lerner, 1991)
Describes groundwater locations and properties, the uses and abuses of it worldwide, and ways to preserve this valuable resource through helpful, easy-to-read text and photographs. (Also available: *Our Endangered Planet: Oceans,* 1991; *Rivers and Lakes,* 1991.)

I/U *The Living Ocean,* by Elizabeth Collins (Chelsea House, 1994)
Gives information on the ever-changing oceanscape, ocean ecosystems, and managing the resources of the oceans.

I/U *Rivers and Lakes,* by Theodore Rowland-Entwistle (Silver Burdett, 1987)
Examines different kinds of rivers and lakes and their importance to plant, animal, and human life surrounding them. Concise text and helpful illustrations.

I/U *Rivers and Lakes,* by Jenny Mulherin (Franklin Watts, 1990)
Descriptions of rivers and lakes around the world, including the wildlife and people on each continent.

I/U *Rivers and People,* by Tom Browne (Silver Burdett, 1982)
Illustrations and photographs, with a thorough text, look at rivers and how the nature of the surroundings has governed man's development and thoughts.

■ Reading Selections

Books marked with an asterisk (*) before and after the title are related to activities in the activity sections of this chapter.

Abel's Island, by William Steig (Farrar, Straus & Giroux, 1986)
>Abel's mouse world has always been a secure place to live until flood waters carry him off and dump him on an uninhabited island. (Chapter Book)

The Adventures of Huckleberry Finn, by Mark Twain (Penguin, 1986)
> Huck floats down the Mississippi with a runaway slave and has many adventures. (Chapter Book)

Ben's Dream, by Chris Van Allsburg (Houghton Mifflin, 1982)
> When a river floods, Ben dreams that he and his house float by the monuments of the world.

Boats, by Byron Barton (Thomas Y. Crowell, 1987)
> Simple text depicts a variety of boats and ships.

Box Turtle at Long Pond, by William T. George (Greenwillow, 1989)
> Follows the day of a box turtle who lives at Long Pond.

By the Shores of Silver Lake, by Laura Ingalls Wilder (Harper, 1953)
> Ma and the girls travel west and live in a railroad camp as they plan for their own home. (Chapter Book)

Dawn, by Uri Shulevitz (Farrar, Straus & Giroux, 1974)
> A man and his grandson watch as dawn breaks over a lake they are camping near.

The Deep Blue Sea, by Bijou Le Tord (Bantam Doubleday Dell, 1996)
> Reflects on God's creation of the mountains, deserts, streams, rivers, and all of the world.

Face to Face, by Marion Dane Bauer (Clarion Books, 1991)
> Michael confronts his fears when he makes a visit to his father in Colorado and joins him on a whitewater rafting trip. (Chapter Book)

Ferryboat, by Betsy Maestro and Giulio Maestro (HarperCollins, 1987)
> Discusses how a ferryboat takes cars back and forth across the river.

Follow the River, by Lydia Dabcovich (Sundance, 1995)
> Follows a stream as it flows through the mountains and countryside until it becomes a river and flows into the ocean.

The Gift of the Willows, by Helena Clare Pittman (Carolrhoda Books, 1988)
> A Japanese couple help two willow trees growing by their home at the river's edge and receive help in return.

I Tell a Lie Every So Often, by Bruce Clements (Farrar, Straus & Giroux, 1984)
> A 14-year-old in the 1840s tells two lies that cause an unusual chain of events. (Chapter Book)

Letting Swift River Go, by Jane Yolen (Little, Brown, 1995)
> A small village sacrifices its town so that a reservoir can be made to furnish water for the city people.

The Little Red Lighthouse and the Great Gray Bridge, by Hildegarde H. Swift and Lynd Ward (Harcourt Brace, 1988)
> After a huge bridge with a searchlight is built next to it, the little red lighthouse thinks that it is no longer useful. However, it finds out that it is still as necessary as ever.

The Lost Lake, by Allen Say (Houghton Mifflin, 1989)
> A young boy and his father plan a quiet trip to Lost Lake, only to find the lake is noisy and overrun with visitors. As the two continue to search for their own special place, they grow closer and build a special bond.

Minn of the Mississippi, by Holling C. Holling (Houghton Mifflin, 1978)
> The adventures of a snapping turtle traveling downstream are used to tell the history of the Mississippi River Valley. (Chapter Book)

On My Honor, by Marion Dane Bauer (Houghton Mifflin, 1987)
> Joel feels horror and guilt after his best friend drowns while they are swimming in a forbidden river near their home. (Chapter Book)

On the Banks of Plum Creek, by Laura Ingalls Wilder (Harper, 1953)
> The Ingallses move to Minnesota and face many misfortunes as they attempt to build a new home. (Chapter Book)

Paddle-to-the-Sea, by Holling C. Holling (Houghton Mifflin, 1980)
> A young Indian boy carves a canoe and journeys in it through the Great Lakes to the Atlantic Ocean. (Chapter Book)

Rain, Rain Rivers, by Uri Shulevitz (Farrar, Straus & Giroux, 1988)
> A child indoors watches the rain on the window and in the streets and tells how it falls on the fields, hills, and seas.

The River, by Gary Paulsen (Yearling Books, 1991)
> Brian, a 15-year-old, is asked to perform a scientific experiment to learn more about the psychology of survival. (Chapter Book)

A River Dream, by Allen Say (Houghton Mifflin, 1988)
> Mark goes on a fantastic fishing trip thanks to a special gift he receives from his uncle when Mark is sick.

Streams to the River, River to the Sea: A Novel of Sacagawea, by Scott O'Dell (Fawcett Books, 1988)
> A young Indian woman experiences an unusual adventure when she joins Lewis and Clark in seeking a path across the country to the Pacific Ocean. (Chapter Book)

Taking Care of Carruthers, by James Marshall (Houghton Mifflin, 2000)
> Eugene and Emily try to cheer up their friend, Carruthers, with a tale about a wonderful afternoon spent on the river.

Three Days on a River in a Red Canoe, by Vera B. Williams (Greenwillow, 1984)
> Two children go canoeing with their mom and aunt and learn many survival skills. Readers are given illustrations and recipes to learn the skills as well.

The Umbrella Day, by Nancy Evans Cooney (Putnam Publishing Group, 1992)
> Missy is glad her mother made her bring her umbrella along when she sees all the wonderful adventures she has with it.

The Unicorn and the Lake, by Marianna Mayer (E. P. Dutton, 1987)
> The unicorn must save all the animals after a snake poisons the lake that they drink from.

Voyage of the Frog, by Gary Paulsen (Orchard, 1989)
> While stranded at sea, David sorts out his feelings about life and his recently departed uncle. (Chapter Book)

What the Dickens!, by Jane Louise Curry (McElderry Books, 1991)
> While living on a canal boat, 11-year-old twins discover a plot to steal the works of Charles Dickens. (Chapter Book)

Where the River Begins, by Thomas Locker (Puffin, 1993)
> When two young boys and their grandfather go on a camping trip, they try to find the source of the river that runs past their home.

Windcatcher, by Avi (Simon & Schuster, 1991)
> While learning to sail, a young boy becomes intrigued over rumors of a sunken treasure. (Chapter Book)

The following books are out of print, but may be available at the local library.

Beside the Bay, by Sheila White Samton (Philomel, 1987)
> A child taking a walk along the bay is joined by a boisterous group of companions.

Canoeing, by Laura Lattig-Ehlers (Picture Book Studios, 1986)
> Describes the sights and sounds while journeying down a river at dusk.

The Cow Who Fell in the Canal, by Phyllis Krasilovsky (Harper & Row, 1988)
> Hendrika, the cow, falls into a canal and floats down to the city to see the sights.

Dark and Full of Secrets, by Carol Carrick (Clarion Books, 1984)
> A boy who drifts too far into the pond and panics when he can't touch the bottom is saved by his dog.

The Frog Who Drank the Waters of the World, by Patricia Montgomery Newton (Atheneum, 1983)
> An old Indian tale about a frog who, for revenge, decides to drink all the water that exists in the forest.

Good Morning, River, by Lisa Westberg Peters (Arcade, 1990)
> Katherine and her friend celebrate the seasons while traveling their river.

Half-a-Button, by Lyn Littlefield Hoopes (Harper & Row, 1989)
> William and his parents sail across the bay to surprise Grampa. Grampa and William spend the day exploring at the water's edge.

The Molasses Flood, by Blair Lent (Houghton Mifflin, 1992)
> After a tank filled with molasses bursts, Charlie Muldon takes a fantastic ride down the streets of Boston on top of his house.

Mr. Bear's Boat, by Thomas Graham (E. P. Dutton, 1988)
> Mr. and Mrs. Bear's first ride in their new boat is not what they had envisioned.

River Friends, by Kathleen M. Kelly (Atheneum, 1988)
> Rusty learns that it can be fun to share the special world that he has always considered his own with a friend.

River Runaways, by David Roth (Houghton Mifflin, 1981)
> Two 14-year-old boys take a canoe down the river to seek their fortunes. (Chapter Book)

Snowy, by Berlie Doherty (HarperCollins, 1993)
> A child feels left out when she can't bring her pet horse to school because the horse must work to pull the barges along the canal.

Tattie's River Journey, by Shirley Rousseau Murphy (Dial Press, 1983)
> Tattie ends up having a wonderful ride when her house floats away on a flooded river.

Tiddalick the Frog, by Susan Nunes (Atheneum, 1989)
> The retelling of a folk tale about a frog who awakes one morning, grumpy and thirsty, and drinks all the freshwater of the world.

Water's Way, by Lisa Westberg Peters (Arcade, 1991)
> Introduces the different forms that water can take, from clouds, to bodies of water, to fog and steam.

■ Science Activities

Riverboats

- Have students research riverboats and answer the following questions: What different types of boats existed? Who invented the steamwheeler? What roles or needs did the riverboats fulfill? Are any still in operation today? If so, what functions do they serve now?

- As a class, design and name your own riverboat (on paper or as an actual model), or re-create one of the riverboats from years gone by.

Water Power

The current of a river or waterfall can be very strong and powerful. Ask the students: How do we harness this energy, and how do we use it? How was this energy harnessed many years ago? Find out if there is an old mill near you that still operates today. If so, plan a trip to see what part water plays in its operation.

Flotation

- What types of objects float in water? Ask the students to gather many different types of objects, then predict whether these objects will float or sink in water and record their predictions. Have them test their theories in a bowl full of water. Use the predictions and results to create math problems for your students.

- Place an unopened can of sugar-free cola and an unopened can of regular cola in the water at the same time. Ask the students to explain why one of the cans floats and the other sinks. (The presence of sugar affects the density of the cola.)

- Have the class design sailboats, or other types of boats, out of the odds and ends you have on hand. Tell them to try to pick out materials that they think will float and then try to sail their vessels. How did they do?

Continental Divide

Ask the students to explain what the Continental Divide is and how it got its name. Have them draw a map that shows where the Continental Divide is located and the paths of water going from the Continental Divide into the major rivers.

Name That Body of Water

- Test your students' knowledge of bodies of water by playing a game. Divide them into two groups (or have them play individually). Ask each group or individual to give the name of a river. Each correct answer scores one point. Each pass or incorrect answer results in no point. See how many rivers can be named.

- Continue the game by moving on to lakes and seas. As a tiebreaker, you can name a body of water and have participants locate it on a map.
- The game can be played with younger students by providing them with a map and asking them to find the bodies of water you name.

Flooding

- Have students do some research to find out what can happen when a river overflows its banks. What type of damage can be done? Give them newspaper clippings and magazine articles about the 1993 Mississippi River flood and have them prepare a script of their findings in the form of a television newscast.
- To enhance their presentations, students should graph the rainfall and river depth at different stages of the flood. Students could also prepare visuals by drawing flood scenes or cutting out pictures from a magazine or newspaper and mounting them on cardboard. Have them prepare questions and interview different people asking them to respond as if they were victims of the flood. If possible, videotape their presentations to simulate a "real" television report.
- If you live near a river, have students research a past flooding of the river. They might be able to find neighbors or relatives who lived through the experience. If you do not live near a river, show the class the portion of the movie *The River* that shows the river flooding and have them prepare their scripts from those sequences.

Canals

- Ask the students: You've heard of the canals of Venice, Italy, but did you know that canals played an important part in the settling of the United States? An entire network of canals was built in the United States in the early 1800s. What purpose did those canals serve?
- Have the students research several famous canals (or a canal that exists, or once existed, near you) and answer these questions: How long did it take to build the canals? How were they built? What purpose were they built for? Are the canals still in use?

Rivers and History

Have the students research the importance of the Mississippi and Ohio rivers in the westbound exploration of the United States and answer these questions: Why were river rights so important to early settlers? What role did rivers play in the French and Indian War? Which "side" of the dispute that caused the war do you agree with? Write an essay supporting your convictions.

Water Supplies

Many towns and cities depend on lakes and reservoirs for their water supply. Ask students how much of that water they think a family would use in a one-week period. Have them find out by using the following chart to monitor their families' water use for 24 hours. They should total the gallons of water used and multiply by seven to determine approximately how much water the family uses in one week. They will need to factor in activities such as clothes and dish washing if none took place on the day they monitored.

Flushing toilet	5 gallons
Showering	30 gallons
Brushing teeth	1 gallon
Bathing	40 gallons
Hand washing dishes	15 gallons

Running dishwasher	30 gallons
Running washing machine	30 gallons
Washing car	20 gallons
Watering lawn (one-half hour)	240 gallons

Have the students use these guidelines to determine the number of gallons used for any other water-related activity that their families participated in while they were monitoring them.

Freshwater Versus Saltwater

- Although 75 percent of the Earth is covered by water, very little of it is freshwater. To demonstrate the proportions of saltwater versus freshwater, measure one gallon of water (16 cups) into a bowl or pan. This represents the Earth's waters.
- Remove 5 tablespoons plus 1/2 teaspoon and place it in a separate container. This represents the Earth's water that is present in icecaps and glaciers.
- Remove another 1 tablespoon plus 2 teaspoons of the 16 cups of water. Place this water in a separate container. This represents the Earth's groundwater. Remove about 8 drops of the original 16 cups of water. This represents the lakes of the world.
- Remove 1 drop for the atmosphere and a very, very small drop for rivers. The remaining 15 1/2 cups plus 1 tablespoon of water represents the oceans. Ask the students what can be said about our freshwater supply.

River Pros and Cons

Discuss rivers. Ask the students: What are rivers used for (water supply, irrigation, fisheries, recreation, shipping, hydroelectricity, transportation, etc.)? What are the advantages and disadvantages of living near a river? Who depends on rivers? Have the students write an essay on whether they would like to live near a river, being sure to include how close to the river they would like to live and the reasoning behind their point of view.

More Flooding

- Discuss the different methods used to attempt to prevent river flooding. Have the students research dredging, building channels, reservoirs, levees, dikes, and river straightening.
- Give the students some modeling clay to use to construct a river scene. They should include a levee, reservoir, and drainage ditch. Have them slowly add water to the river and see how well their structures help retard the flooding.
- Show the class the scene from the movie *The River* in which the townspeople try to hold back the river and protect their farms from flooding. Have the students list problems that can occur when rivers flood.

Water and Gravity

Tell your students that water is pulled toward the center of the Earth, like everything else, by gravity. This can be evidenced by waterfalls. Knowing this, how can they explain the following experiment?

Suck up some water into a straw. Quickly put your finger over the top of the straw. You will notice that the water in the straw does not run out. Hold the straw upright. The water still stays in the straw. Why? (Unless air can get to the top of the straw and break the suction formed by your finger, the water will remain in the straw. The force of the vacuum counteracts the force of gravity.)

■ Creative Writing Activities

Following are instructions to give the students for various writing activities.

- You have been invited by your best friend's family to join them for a day of sailing at a nearby lake. Write a diary entry describing the day and what you enjoyed most. You could also write a funny story about a day of sailing (or boating) filled with mishaps. (*Mr. Bear's Boat* by Graham)

- Write a poem about a babbling brook. Include descriptive words and phrases that bring to mind the sounds of a brook "dancing" over rocks as it flows through a forest.

- Imagine you are riding the rapids during a whitewater river rafting trip in Colorado. Write a story about the adventures you experience. Be sure to include descriptions of your feelings during the trip and of the scenery you travel through.

- What does it mean to be "up a creek without a paddle"? Write a story that includes this saying in its plot.

- Do you have a special place where you go when you need to be by yourself just to think? If not, envision what such a place would be like for you. Write a story about your struggle to decide whether to share your special place with a close friend who seems to need a refuge. (*River Friends* by Kelly)

- You and your friends are building a raft and plan to sail down the river searching for adventure. Write a journal detailing the preparations for your journey and the adventures you have. (*The Adventures of Huckleberry Finn* by Twain)

- Compare and contrast *The Frog Who Drank the Waters of the World* by Newton and *Tiddalick the Frog* by Nunes. Who is credited with writing each of these tales? Give your explanation of how two such similar stories could have such diverse sources.

- Find out what country your ancestors emigrated to America from (if so). See if any relatives have information about what your ancestors' voyage was like and what their early lives in America were like. (If not, read *How Many Days to America* by Bunting.) Pretend you are one of your ancestors (or a character in the story) and write a letter to friends back in the homeland describing what your journey was like.

- Take the class on an outing to a nearby park. After the visit, make a detailed map of the park and the equipment and other landmarks it contains. Using different-colored markers or colored pencils, show the routes you took while playing on the different pieces of equipment or taking part in other activities at the park that day. Create a legend that shows what the different colors you have used denote (first, second, and third activities, etc.). (*Three Days on a River in a Red Canoe* by Williams)

- Write an adventure story about your escapades as you attempt to travel to the source of a mysterious river in the wilds of Africa. (*Where The River Begins* by Locker)

- Make up a fanciful tale about the adventures you experience when your town is flooded by _____. Fill in the blank with your favorite treat (chocolate syrup, pineapple milkshakes, cherry cola, hot fudge, etc.). How did the flood get started? What effect did it have on the town? Was it a fun or gruesome experience? (*The Molasses Flood* by Lent)

- Have you ever thought what it would feel like to be in a situation where you thought you were going to drown? Write a descriptive story that not only gives the details of what happened but also relates how you felt during the time when your life was in peril (*Dark and Full of Secrets* by Carrick). As a follow-up activity, research safe swimming and boating procedures and write a list of safety rules.

■ Art Activities

Following are instructions to give the students for various art activities.

- Draw a picture of an imaginary adventure involving you, your umbrella, and a long, winding river. (*The Umbrella Day* by Cooney)

- Read *Dawn* by Uri Shulevitz. Write your own story about a lake during a particular time of day. Make abstract illustrations of your story similar to the ones in *Dawn*.

- Make a picture, using colored chalk, that depicts the sun rising (or setting) over a mountain lake. What colors would you use? Why? What would be the difference in color choice from sunrise to sunset? Find magazines or books with photographs of both types of scenes and compare them to your artwork.

- Create a scene of a forest that has a pond. Use a strong piece of cardboard covered with foil for the pond. Then be creative. Use real rocks (or make your own out of crumpled newspaper painted brown or gray), make plants out of green tissue paper, use brown construction paper for logs, and so forth.

- Draw a scene that includes a waterfall. Use any medium you want to: paint, chalk, crayon, and so forth. Add strips of foil, colored plastic wrap, or tissue paper to make your waterfall 3-dimensional.

- Find a picture of a child dressed as if he or she could be walking by a brook or creek in a wooded area and pictures of different woodland creatures. On a piece of paper, draw the brook or creek and the surrounding scene. Paste the cutouts on your picture to make a funny scene. What are your child and creatures doing that is so unusual? (*Beside the Bay* by Samton)

- On a piece of 8 1/2-by-11-inch paper, draw six 3-by-3-inch boxes lengthwise (make two rows of three boxes each). Inside each box, draw a different picture depicting a different form that water can take (clouds, rain, rivers, fog, steam, etc.). Try to draw your pictures in sequential order (i.e., if you begin with clouds, move on to a picture of rain, sleet, or snow, then draw a picture of a body of water, etc.). *(Water's Way* by Peters)

- Make a mosaic scene focusing on a lake or river. Cut small shapes out of construction paper, wrapping or tissue paper, fabric, or magazine pictures. Assemble the shapes to make a picture of your pond, lake, or river scene.

- Construct a raft out of ice cream or Popsicle sticks:

    Make the floor of the raft by laying 12 or 13 sticks side-by-side on a flat surface. Leave enough space between the sixth and seventh sticks to wedge in a stick (standing upright) to use as the mast for the sail.

    Lay six sticks, lengthwise, across the original sticks and glue them in place. These six sticks will hold your floor together.

    Place one stick, upright, through the space you left in the floor to serve as the mast. On the underside of the raft, glue two more sticks (that run the same way as the floor) on either side of the part of the mast that is sticking through the floor. This will help reinforce the mast and allow it to stand up.

    Cut a piece of paper in the size and shape that you want for your sail. Decorate it.

    Cut a small slit in the middle of the sail about 1 inch from the top and another slit 1 inch from the bottom. Slip the mast through the slits in the sail, and your raft is complete.

- Make a river scene that shows a person fishing from a boat as he or she floats on the water:

  Use a paper plate as your water. Color an underwater scene (fish, plants, rocks, etc.) on the right-hand side of the paper plate with crayons.

  Paint over your drawing with blue watercolors to make the scene appear to be underwater.

  Cut a strip out of poster board that is 1 inch wide and about 5 1/2 inches long. The strip should reach from the center of the plate to about 2 inches past the edge of the plate.

  Draw a picture on poster board of a rowboat with a person inside holding a fishing pole. The picture should be about 3 inches by 3 inches. Color the picture and cut it out.

  Poke a hole in the center of the plate and another one about 1/2 inch from one end of the strip.

  Attach the strip to the back of the plate with a brass fastener.

  Poke a hole through the center of your boat and another one about 1/2 inch from the other end of the strip.

  Attach the ship to the strip, so that the decorated side of the boat faces your underwater scene, with a brass fastener. As you move the strip of poster board around, your boat will appear to be moving across the water. The person on board will look as though he or she is fishing.

Chapter 3
Oceans

■ Teaching Resources

Books continuing experiment(s) relating to the subject matter are marked with a plus sign (+) before and after the title.

P   *Follow the Water from Brook to Ocean,* by Arthur Dorros (Harper Trophy, 1993)
Through simple text and illustrations, follows water, which begins as a brook and travels on to the ocean..

P   *From Sea to Salt,* by Ali Mitgutsch (Carolrhoda Books, 1985)
Simple illustrations and text to describe salt extraction from mines and the sea.

P/I *Look Inside the Ocean,* by Laura Crema (Grosset & Dunlap, 1998)
Uses a question-and-answer format with enjoyable illustrations about ocean life.

P/I *+River and Oceans,+* by Barbara Taylor (Kingfisher Books, 1993)
Geography facts and experiments introduce the different forms of water in our world, the water cycle, stages of a river, currents, lakes, and pollution.

PI/U *Coral Reef Images,* by Michael George (Creative Editions, 1992)
Beautiful, full-color pages with brief text overlaid that describes coral reef formation and animals that live there.

PI/U *+ Marine Biology,+* by Ellen Doris (Thames & Hudson, 1993)
Done in connection with Woods Hole, Massachusetts, Children's School of Science, this book describes coastal waters, with nice photographs and clear text.

I   *The Magic School Bus on the Ocean Floor,* by Joanna Cole (Scholastic, 1994)
With enlightening illustrations, Ms. Frizzle leads her class on an ocean tour, explaining it and the creatures who live there.

I   *Oceans,* by Seymour Simon (Mulberry Press, 1997)
Brilliant photographs, with brief text, describe the physical characteristics, life, and fragility of the world's oceans.

I   *The Sea,* by Brian Williams (Kingfisher Books, 1992)
A colorful volume that covers ocean formation, animal and plant life, and technology used to explore the ocean.

I   *+The Young Scientist Book of the Undersea,+* by Christopher Pick (EMC Corporation, 1978)
Brief explanations of marine animals, underwater exploration, treasure hunting, fish, and plant life.

I/U *Oceans, Our Endangered Planet,* by Mary Hoff and Mary M. Rodgers (Lerner, 1992)
Concise text, with helpful, color photographs, looking at our uses and abuses of the world's seas and oceans.

I/U *Protecting the Oceans,* by John Baines (Steck-Vaughn, 1991)
Numerous illustrations and concise text describe the importance of oceans, the pollution and misuse of them, and ways to protect them.

I/U *Seas and Oceans,* by David Lambert (Raintree Steck Vaughn, 1994)
Brief text and nice photographs describe the oceans of the world, their physical features, plant and animal life, and what the future holds.

U *Diving into Darkness,* by Rebecca L. Johnson (Lerner, 1989)
Up-to-date book with color photographs. Looks at work done by submersibles, especially the Johnson Sea Link sub, to explore the ocean depths, and what they find.

U *The Great Barrier Reef,* by Rebecca L. Johnson (Lerner, 1991)
Beautiful photographs help explain research projects at Australia's Great Barrier Reef involving animals and plants.

■ Reading Selections

Books marked with an asterisk (*) before and after the title are related to activities in the activity sections of this chapter.

Alec's Sand Castle, by Lavinia Russ (Harper & Row, 1972)
When the adults begin to take over the building of his sand castle, Alec begins another one that only he can construct.

At the Beach, by Anne Rockwell and Harlow Rockwell (Aladdin, 1991)
Recounts the sights and sounds that a child enjoys during a day spent at the beach.

Beach Ball, by Peter Sis (Greenwillow, 1990)
A lost beach ball leads the reader on a search for letters, numbers, shapes, and opposites. (Wordless Book)

Boat Book, by Gail Gibbons (Holiday House, 1988)
Introduces children to many different boats that sail on the oceans.

Boats, by Byron Barton (HarperCollins, 1998)
Simple text depicts a variety of boats and ships.

A Boy's Will, by Erik Christian Haugaard (Houghton Mifflin, 1990)
Patrick risks everything to warn John Paul Jones about an English ambush of the American fleet. (Chapter Book)

Brambly Hedge Sea Story, by Jill Barklem (Atheneum, 2000)
The residents of Brambly Hedge find that sailing a boat is not as easy as they thought. They end up having a much bigger adventure than they anticipated.

By the Sea, by Mary Hofstrand (Simon & Schuster, 1989)
A young pig tells how his daily life changes when his parents take him to the seashore.

Come a Tide, by George Ella Lyon (Orchard, 1993)
> Cheerful illustrations depict the doughty neighborliness of rumpled folk as they cope with floodwaters and torrential rains.

Curious George at the Beach, by Margret Rey and Alan J. Shalleck (Houghton Mifflin, 1999)
> Although George gets into his usual amount of trouble while spending a day at the beach, he also ends up saving someone's life.

Devil Storm, by Theresa Nelson (Universe, 2000)
> Tom the Tramp becomes a great hero after the Storm of 1900. (Chapter Book)

*D.W. All Wet,** by Marc Brown (Little, Brown, 1991)
> Arthur's little sister spends her first day at the beach resisting her family's efforts to get her into the water.

Four Brave Sailors, by Mirra Ginsburg (Greenwillow, 1987)
> Four mice prove to be brave sailors who are afraid of nothing but a cat.

Goodbye, Vietnam, by Gloria Whelan (Random House , 1993)
> A young girl and her family make a perilous journey from Vietnam to Hong Kong by sea to escape the brutal government. (Chapter Book)

*How Many Days to America?,** by Eve Bunting (Clarion Books, 1990)
> Refugees who embark on a dangerous ocean voyage to America have a very special reason to celebrate Thanksgiving.

Ice Swords—An Undersea Adventure, by James Houston (McClelland and Stewart, 1986)
> As two boys help a scientist in the Arctic dive under the sea ice and photograph whales, they fail to see the danger that approaches them. (Chapter Book)

The Jolly Mon, by Jimmy Buffett and Savannah Jane Buffett (Harcourt Brace, 1993)
> Jolly Mon finds a magical guitar in the sea. In a boat built for him by the people of Bananaland, he journeys out to share his music with the world.

Little Tim and the Brave Sea Captain, by Edward Ardizzone (HarperCollins, 2000)
> Tim stows away on a great steamer going out to sea. When a storm hits, his adventures turn out to be more than he bargained for.

The Maggie B., by Irene Haas (Macmillan, 1975)
> A little girl goes on a voyage with a new friend in a boat that is named for her.

Ocean Day, by Shelley Rotner and Ken Kreisler (Macmillan, 1993)
> Emily takes a trip to the ocean and learns many things about the seashore and the creatures who live there.

An Ocean World, by Peter Sis (HarperCollins, 2000)
> Generally wordless, this picture book follows a captive whale that is released into the open seas.

Oh, Brother, by Arthur Yorinks and Richard Egielski (Farrar, Straus & Giroux, 1989)
> An accident at sea strands two bratty brothers in New York. Through hardships and difficulties, they work their way up to the positions of "Royal Tailors" and are reunited with their parents.

The Owl and the Pussycat, by Edward Lear (Putnam, 1991)
> The classic tale of an unusual romance between an owl and a pussycat who set sail one night.

Pagoo, by Holling C. Holling (Houghton Mifflin, 1990)
> A study of tide pools as seen through the eyes of Pagoo, a hermit crab.

Reflections, by Ann Jonas (Greenwillow Books, 1987)
> Follows a child's day by the sea. The pictures change when the book is turned upside down.

Riptide, by Frances Weller (Philomel, 1990)
> Riptide, a dog, becomes the 19th lifeguard on Nauset Beach.

Sailing with the Wind, by Thomas Locker (Dial Books for Young Readers, 1993)
> A young girl takes a sailing trip with her uncle and sees the majesty of the ocean.

Sailor Bear, by Martin Waddell (Econo-Clad, 1999)
> A little lost bear tries, unsuccessfully, to be a sailor and sail the sea, but ends up right where he belongs.

Sea and I, by Harutaka Nakawatari (Farrar, Straus & Giroux, 1994)
> A son is afraid for his father, who is out on the water in a fierce storm, but is calmed by observing nature around him.

Seabird, by Holling C. Holling (Houghton Mifflin, 1978)
> This book presents a history of America at sea as seen through the travels of a carved ivory seabird.

The Seashore Book, by Charlotte Zolotow (HarperCollins, 1992)
> A mother describes the sights and sounds of the seashore to her young son, who has never seen the ocean.

Sheep on a Ship, by Nancy Shaw (Houghton Mifflin, 1989)
> Sheep take a voyage on the sea, only to meet with a fierce storm. They are all happy to make it back to port. Text presented in a tongue-twister style.

Voyage of the Frog, by Gary Paulsen (Orchard, 1989)
> David is out on the sea in a fierce storm and must survive for several days on his own. (Chapter Book)

Watch the Stars Come Out, by Riki Levinson (Puffin, 1995)
> Grandma tells her grandchildren how her mother came across the ocean to America in a big boat.

When the Tide Is Low, by Sheila Cole (Morrow, 1985)
> A little girl and her mother eagerly await all the wonderful things they will do when the tide lowers.

Where Does the Trail Lead?, by Burton Albert (Simon & Schuster, 1991)
> A young boy follows an island trail by the sea through flowers and dunes to find out where the trail finally leads.

Why the Tides Ebb and Flow, by Joan Bowden (Houghton Mifflin, 1990)
> A folk tale in which an old woman threatens to pull the rock from the hole in the ocean floor.

Worse Than Willy!, by James Stevenson (Greenwillow, 1987)
> Grandpa tells Mary Ann and Louie a seafaring story about the problems his brother, Wainey, caused when he was little.

The Wreck of the Zephyr, by Chris Van Allsburg (Houghton Mifflin, 1983)
> A tale of a boy who learns to sail above the water, but no one believes his story.

The following books are out of print, but may be available at the local library.

Beach Days, by Ken Robbins (Viking Kestrel, 1987)
> A trip to the beach is recalled through photographs and simple text in poetic form.

How the Sea Began, by George Crespo (Houghton Mifflin, 1993)
> A folk tale of the Taino people of Puerto Rico that explains how the sea came into being.

Laffite the Pirate, by Ariane Dewey (Greenwillow, 1985)
> Tells several tales about the infamous pirate Jean Laffite.

The Man Whose Mother Was a Pirate, by Margaret Mahy (Puffin Books, 1987)
> A little man sets off on a journey to take his mother, who used to be a pirate, back to the sea.

The Old Ball and the Sea, by Warren Gebert (Bradbury Press, 1988)
> A boy and his dog spend their day at the beach playing in the sand and with a ball that washes ashore.

The Stowaway, by James Stevenson (Greenwillow, 1990)
> A young mouse, crossing the ocean for the first time on a cruise liner, helps a stowaway avoid capture.

The Turtle Watchers, by Pamela Powell (Viking, 1992)
> Three sisters on an island work together to save leatherback turtles from poachers. (Chapter Book)

■ Science Activities

A New World

Listed below are several groups of people who crossed the ocean and came to a new land. Have students pick one of the examples and delve deeper into it. They should prepare a report on the subject. Have them interview people who fit in the category or whose ancestors did. Students should answer the questions listed for each group in their reports. Also have them prepare charts of the course the ships took from Europe, Africa, or Asia to the United States.

- The Pilgrims—Where did they come from? When did they travel to America? Why did they leave their homeland? How long did their voyage across the ocean take? What was their voyage like? How many people set out on the *Mayflower* and how many actually made it to the New World?

- The Slaves—Many slaves were shipped across the ocean to market in the United States. What time frame are we considering here? What would a slave's voyage have been like? In your report, consider how our country would have been different if there had been no slavery. Also, research the contributions that black Americans have made to our society.

- The Immigrants—When did the largest immigration to the United States occur? What countries contributed most of the immigrants? Why did these people choose to come to the United States? This category covers a wide variety of types of ocean voyages. Compare and contrast some of them. Did the immigrants have to meet any requirements before they were allowed access to the United States? Were immigrants ever denied access and made to return to their home country?

Saltwater

How can you show that the sea has salt? Give students pie pans and a small amount of "seawater," or salty water if no ocean water is readily available. Place the pans in sunlight or near a heater vent and let the water evaporate. Examine the substance that is left. You will find that it does have a salty taste. Explain to the students that water flows over land and brings minerals from the land to the ocean. Through the water cycle, the water goes back to the land in the form of rain and leaves the minerals behind in the ocean water. These minerals keep getting stronger (more concentrated) as the process repeats.

Let a can of frozen orange juice melt completely. Have students taste the concentrated liquid. This is orange juice in its most concentrated form, similar to the minerals concentrated in seawater.

More Saltwater

Have students use modeling clay to make shapes, then see if they float in water, and ask them which shapes float best. Then place these shapes in saltwater and ask the students how well they float in that water. Make a list of the possible advantages and disadvantages of the ocean being saltwater.

Making Waves

For this demonstration, you'll need a tall, narrow bottle with a tight-fitting cap, cooking oil, water, and blue food coloring. Have a student fill the bottle one fourth of the way with water and add a drop of blue or green food coloring, shaking it to mix. Then have another student fill the bottle to the top with cooking oil or baby oil, leaving no room at the top for air, and screw the cap back on as tightly as possible. Ask a third student to lay the bottle on a table and gently roll it back and forth. Tell the class to watch the blue water move back and forth just like ocean waves. Shake the bottle and watch little bubbles form as if on a stormy sea.

Rock the Boat

Water on the surface of an ocean moves up and down. The water does not actually move forward until it reaches the shore. Try this simple experiment to demonstrate this process:

- Ask a student to tie one end of a thin rope (about 13 feet long) to a tree or post at the same height as his or her waistline, then hold on to the other end of the rope and stand about 10 feet away from the tree or post.
- Have the student shake the rope up and down, quickly. Draw the class's attention to the way a wave moves along the rope, but the rope itself does not move forward.

Students can do another experiment at home to demonstrate this fact:

- Fill a washtub about two-thirds full of water. Gently disturb the water by using an eggbeater (NOT an electric mixer) to make waves. Observe the pattern of the waves as they move outward.
- Float a cork in the water, then drop in a stone. The cork will bob up and down because of the movement of the waves caused by the stone, but the cork does not move closer to the edge of the tub.

Bermuda Triangle

Have students research legends surrounding the Bermuda Triangle and identify some of the scientific theories that could explain this phenomenon. Have them write a paper presenting their theories of what might be causing these mysterious events or why they believe that no such events have really actually taken place. Remind them to be sure to include facts to back up their theories.

Ocean Versus Sea

Ask the students to explain the difference between an ocean and a sea. Have them locate different oceans and seas on a world map and answer these questions: Is there a visible difference between the oceans and seas? How many oceans are there? Are there seven seas, as stories often mention?

Ocean Resources

Ask the students to name the resources we get from the ocean and speculate about who owns these resources. Have them research the laws on maritime rights and identify which resources from the ocean are considered most valuable.

Ocean Currents

Find a map showing principal ocean currents of the world. You can write to the U.S. Department of Commerce for a map. (The address is included in the "Additional Resources" section of this unit.) Have the students find the following currents and research the path and direction(s) of the currents:

North Equatorial	Alaska
South Equatorial	Norwegian
West Wind Drift	Agulhas
East Greenland	Benguela
Equatorial Counter	Antilles
Falkland	Brazil

On the Beach

Compare and contrast the two types of sand: biological (from the breakdown of sea animals, skeletons, shells, coral, etc.) and nonbiological (from weathering and erosion of rocks). Ask the students: How do the two types differ in consistency? How do they differ in appearance? As a class, speculate about why different beaches are different colors. For example, what forms the black beaches in Hawaii or the white beaches in the Caribbean? You can also obtain sea shells of various sizes and shapes and use them as math manipulatives, to teach sequencing, to reinforce measuring skills, and so forth.

■ Creative Writing Activities

Following are instructions to give the students for various writing activities.

- Have you ever been afraid of something only to find that, once you tried it, you loved it? Write a letter to a friend describing such an experience and telling what happened. (*D. W. All Wet* by Brown)
- You are walking along the beach when you see a trail to your left leading away from the shore. You follow it. Where does the trail take you? What do you see? Write a story for a neighborhood newspaper telling other residents what they can see if they follow the trail (*Where Does The Trail Lead?* by Albert). Older students can also make a map of the trail showing where sights of interest can be found.
- You are walking along the beach as the tide is coming in. You look down to find an unusual object being washed ashore. What is the object? Where did it come from? What is the result of your discovery? Write a story encompassing the points listed above (and more, if you want). (*The Old Ball and the Sea* by Gebert)

- What would it have been like to travel, as a child your age, across the ocean to a new land to start a new life? Write a diary about your journey and your feelings as you take this momentous trip into the unknown. (*Watch the Stars Come Out* by Levinson; *How Many Days to America?* by Bunting)

- All oceans have currents. Scientists often throw bottles into the ocean to track the currents. Bottles have also been thrown into the ocean to signal for help. Look on a world map and choose an island. Pretend you are shipwrecked on that island. Write a message to place in a bottle. Be sure your message describes where you are: your latitude and longitude, the climate, what plant and animal life is present on the island, and any other distinguishing factors.

- Throughout history many ships have been wrecked and have sunk to the ocean floor. Write a story about your adventures as part of an expedition searching for and raising a ship from the ocean floor. How do you determine where to look? What process do you use to actually raise the ship? What "treasures" do you find?

- What would happen to the world if the oceans dried up? Write a science fiction story in which the oceans are mysteriously evaporating. What is the cause? Is there anything you can do to remedy the situation?

- Write a tall tale to explain why the ocean is salty.

- Find out what country your ancestors emigrated to America from (if so). See if any relatives have information on what your ancestors' voyage was like and what their early lives in America were like. (If not, read *How Many Days to America?* by Bunting.) Pretend you are one of your ancestors (or a character in the story) and write a letter to friends back in the homeland describing what your journey was like.

- Legend has it that many ships have been lost, and never seen again, after entering the Bermuda Triangle. Locate this area on a map and familiarize yourself with some of its legends. Then write your own account of a ship traveling through this eerie spot.

- In Columbus's time, sailors believed that the world was flat. If you sailed too far in any one direction, you would fall off of the edge of the world. Imagine you are a sailor setting out with Columbus in search of a new trade route to the East. Keep a daily log of your voyage. Include in your log your feelings about the journey both before you start out and as it drags on week after week.

- There have been many myths about giant sea monsters that inhabit the seas and wreak havoc on ships as they sail the oceans. Imagine you are a sailor traveling on a large schooner that comes face-to-face with a giant sea serpent. Write an account of your encounter with this mythical beast.

■ Art Activities

Following are instructions to give the students for various art activities.

- Read *Laffite the Pirate* by Dewey, or any other pirate story. When you finish the story, design your own pirate hat out of newspaper that you paint or out of construction paper. You can also make a patch for your eye with some elastic sewn to black cloth or black construction paper and string. Find clothes around the house that remind you of the clothes pirates would wear. Make your costume as intricate or as simple as you want. Put on a play that re-creates your favorite scene from the pirate book you read, or work in a group with other students to make up a story for the play.

- Draw, or paint, a beach scene. You can make a deserted beach with just the scenery, a picture of people swimming, a beach house, and so forth. Put down a piece of newspaper (to help keep the mess to a minimum) and put glue on the parts of the picture that you would like to cover with sand. (You might want to glue just one section of the picture at a time so you won't have to rush.) Sprinkle sand over the glue, pat it down lightly with your fingertips, and let it dry. Add color to the sand by lightly painting watercolors over the sand when it has dried. (*Reflections* by Jonas; *By the Sea* by Hofstrand, *Beach Days* by Robbins; *At the Beach* by Rockwell and Rockwell)

- Make a collage of ocean scenes. Cut out pictures from magazines and periodicals that show ocean scenes and glue them to a large piece of poster board. Think of a title for your creation that impresses upon others the ocean's beauty and power.

- Use wet paper and watercolors to make a picture of the ocean. Wet a piece of industrial-strength paper towel or a double thickness of regular paper towel. Choose your colors and paint your ocean on the paper towels with watercolors. As you paint, the watercolors will be absorbed by the paper towel and spread through your picture. When you have finished, place the picture in a safe place to dry.

- To make your own sea shells out of paper, color an 8 1/2-by-11-inch piece of paper (this will make two shells) widthwise in yellow, black, and brown stripes. Cut the paper diagonally into two pieces. Roll each piece of paper into a cone and tape or glue it together securely.

- Create sand art using the following process:

    You'll need nine empty glass jars or bottles, with lids (one of these may be larger or a special shape), several colors of powder paints, a funnel (optional, but helpful), and sand (enough to fill all nine jars or bottles).

    Fill eight of the jars halfway with sand.

    Choose a color of powder paint and pour some of it into one of the jars. Cover the jar tightly and shake it well. This will color your sand. Repeat this procedure, using a different color paint, with each of the remaining jars.

    Take the empty container (the special-shaped one) and begin pouring the different colors of sand into it. Start with one color and pour 1 inch of sand into the bottle. Choose another color and pour 1/2 inch of sand on top of the first layer. Continue doing this, varying the thickness of your layers, until your bottle is full. Along the sides of the jar, you can make indentations with a toothpick and let the sand flow down into the previous layer of sand. Do this after adding each layer of sand.

    Put the lid on the bottle tightly and admire your sand "sculptures."

- Make your own pretend scuba mask to explore the ocean floor. Place a paper grocery bag over your head and have someone mark, on the unprinted side of the bag, approximately where your eyes are. Cut out an oval in this space to serve as the viewing area of your mask. Cover the cut out section with plastic wrap taped to the inside of the bag. Tape an empty paper towel roll to one side of the oval to serve as your breathing tube. Decorate your scuba mask however you wish.

- Make a cockle or scallop shell by coloring an 8 1/2-by-11-inch piece of paper, widthwise, pink, yellow, purple, red, and brown. Blend the colors into each other. Fold the paper accordion-style; then open and flatten the sheet of paper. Trim the corners of the paper to round them. Pinch one of the long edges of the paper together to give your shell some height, then tape it in place.

- To make a limpet shell, color an 8 1/2-by-11-inch sheet of paper, widthwise, brown with small lines of black radiating out from what will be the center of your shell. Trim the corners of the paper so that it is oval shaped. Cut a slit from the middle of one long edge of the paper to the center of the shell. Overlap the edges caused by the slit slightly and glue or tape them into place. Trim the shell if needed to make it the shape you wish.

- Make a pencil holder with an old juice, vegetable, or fruit can and pasta shells. Cover the outside of the can with a piece of colored construction paper. Decorate the pasta shells using magic markers and then glue the shells onto the construction paper in whatever design you want. Use your markers to make additional designs and drawings on the construction paper. Alternatively, glue the undecorated shells directly to the outside of the can and spray paint the entire pencil holder with one or more colors.

- Make a ship in a bottle. Construct your own boat using Styrofoam, Popsicle sticks, fabric, straws, sponges, toothpicks, wood, and similar items. Cut open a plastic, 2-liter bottle all the way down one side. Place the boat inside the bottle and secure it in place with tape or a piece of modeling clay. Tape the side of the bottle shut with transparent tape and replace the cap.

- Draw an underwater scene that includes coral, shells, and small sea creatures. Paint over the shapes you drew with glue or rubber cement. After the glue has dried, paint over the top of the entire picture with watercolors to represent the water. The paint will not stick to the areas covered with glue. If you use rubber cement, rub away the cement to reveal the objects you drew underneath.

- Make textured paintings of the ocean by using materials such as sponges, doilies, feathers, paper wads, and combs. Brush paint onto the items you have chosen, press them against a piece of white (or colored) paper, and then peel them off gently to make your ocean scene.

Chapter 4

Landforms and Geological Processes

■ Teaching Resources

Books containing experiment(s) relating to the subject matter are marked with a plus sign (+) before and after the title.

P *Discover My World,* by Ron Hirschi (Bantam Books, 1992)
Explores a variety of life in the mountains through a question-and-answer format.

P/I *Earthquakes,* by Seymour Simon (Mulberry Books, 1995)
Brief text and excellent photos of causes of earthquakes and their aftermath.

P/I *Look Closer: Cave Life,* by Christiane Gunzi (Dorling Kindersley, 1993)
Brief text on plants and animals in caves, with excellent photos.

P/I *The Magic School Bus Inside the Earth,* by Joanna Cole (Scholastic, 1989)
Follow Ms. Frizzle's class while they learn about different kinds of rocks and the Earth's formations.

P/I *+Mountains and Volcanoes,+* by Barbara Taylor (Kingfisher Books, 1993)
Explores mountain formation, composition, volcanoes, and the erosion process.

P/I *Volcanoes,* by Seymour Simon (Mulberry Books, 1995)
Wonderful photographs and brief text describe volcanoes, including some famous ones and their effects.

P/I *Volcanoes and Earthquakes,* by Zuza Vrbova (Troll, 1990)
Easy format on volcanoes and earthquakes around the world, as well as on other planets.

I *Avalanche,* by Stephen Kramer (Carolrhoda Books, 1992)
Beautiful photography, with concise text about avalanches. It includes information on controlling avalanches and what the aftereffects are.

I *Icebergs and Glaciers,* by Seymour Simon (Mulberry Books, 1999)
Easy-to-read text with excellent photographs describing iceberg and glacier formation and where they are found.

I *Looking Inside Caves and Caverns,* by Ron Schultz (John Muir Publications, 1993)
Cartoon pictures and true-to-life photography accompany a thorough text about caves and caving.

I *Mountains,* by Keith Lye and Karen Johnson (Raintree, 1996)
Describes, with easy-to-read text, different kinds of mountains, including their inhabitants. Includes the need for conservation.

I/U *Avalanche,* by Stephen Kramer (Carolrhoda Books, 1992)
Describes formation, types, and locations of avalanches, as well as safety; includes beautiful photographs.

I/U *Earthquake,* by Christopher Lampton (Millbrook Press, 1994)
Concise information and great photographs explaining causes and results of earthquakes along with methods scientists are using to explore and control them.

I/U *Volcano,* by Christopher Lampton (Econo-Clad, 1999)
Nice photography and concise text describe four types of volcanoes, the causes for their eruptions, and how lava enriches the soil.

■ Reading Selections

Books marked with an asterisk (*) before and after the title are related to activities in the activity sections of this chapter.

Abel's Island, by William Steig (Farrar, Straus & Giroux, 1988)
> Abel's mouse world has always been a secure place to live, until flood waters carry him off and dump him on an uninhabited island. (Chapter Book)

Beady Bear, by Don Freeman (Econo-Clad), 1999
> Beady decides that, to be truly happy, he must go off and find a cave of his own to live in. He soon finds out that he needs more than a cave to find true happiness.

Borrowed Children, by George Ella Lyon (University Press of Kentucky, 1999)
> Amanda gets a vacation from her Kentucky mountain home after serving as mother and housekeeper during her Mama's illness. (Chapter Book)

The Bridge Dancers, by Carol Saller (First Avenue Editions, 1993)
> Maisie uses the knowledge of herbal medicine she learned from her mother, a mountain healer, to help her sister. (Chapter Book)

Canyons, by Gary Paulsen (Delacorte Press, 1990)
> Brennan finds a skull in a canyon near El Paso, Texas, and becomes involved with the fate of an Apache Indian of long ago. (Chapter Book)

Caught in the Moving Mountains, by Gloria Skurzynski (Beachtree Books, 1994)
> While hiking in the mountains, two brothers must fight to survive when they are confronted by an injured drug dealer and caught in an earthquake. (Chapter Book)

Dawn, by Uri Shulevitz (Farrar, Straus & Giroux, 1988)
> A man and his grandson observe the beauty of day breaking over the landscape that surrounds them.

The Empty Island, by Roger Smith (Crocodile Books, 1991)
> When an island couple take on the coats and features of the island animals, they learn a valuable lesson.

Good Times on Grandfather Mountain, by Jacqueline Martin (Orchard, 1992)
> Washburn continues to look on the bright side even when disasters continue to befall him.

Grandpa's Mountain, by Carolyn Reeder (Camelot Books, 1993)
> While Carrie is visiting him, her grandfather is in a desperate fight to keep the government from taking his mountain farm for a park. (Chapter Book)

Hanna's Hog, by Jim Aylesworth (Atheneum, 1988)
> Hanna must find a way to save her chickens and hogs from thieves.

Heidi, by Johanna Spyri (Grammercy, 1998)
> Heidi must leave her mountain home to care for an invalid girl in the city. (Chapter Book)

The Hill and the Rock, by David McKee (Anderson Press, 1999)
> Mr. and Mrs. Quest move the rock that obstructs the view from their hilltop home, only to find that the hill deflates and they are now living in a valley.

The Island, by Gary Paulsen (Econo-Clad, 1999)
> A 15-year-old boy discovers the wonders of nature after leaving home to live on an island off northern Wisconsin. (Chapter Book)

An Island Christmas, by Lynn Joseph (Clarion Books, 1996)
> Preparations for Christmas in Trinidad include picking red petals for the sorrel drink, mixing up the batter for black currant cake, and singing along with the parang (sword) band.

Island of the Blue Dolphins, by Scott O'Dell (Yearling Books, 1987)
> The story of a young Indian girl who survives by herself on a deserted island off the California coast for 18 years. (Chapter Book)

The Island on Bird Street, by Uri Orlev (Econo-Clad, 1990)
> A Jewish boy is left on his own for months in the Warsaw Ghetto during World War II, and he must learn to survive under terrible hardships. (Chapter Book)

It's Mine!, by Leo Lionni (Dragonfly, 1996)
> On an island in the middle of Rainbow Pond live three frogs who quarrel and fight all day long. After they share a fearsome adventure, their attitudes toward each other change.

The Jolly Mon, by Jimmy Buffett and Savannah Jane Buffett (Harcourt Brace, 1993)
> Jolly Mon finds a magical guitar floating in the sea. In a boat built for him by the people of Bananaland, he journeys out to share his music with the world.

The Knight and the Dragon, by Tomie de Paola (Paper Star, 1998)
> A knight in his castle and a dragon in his cave work to prepare for their first meeting.

The Kweeks of Kookatumdee, by Bill Peet (Houghton Mifflin, 1988)
> A group of birdlike creatures are starving because their island does not have enough trees to feed all of them. All seems lost until one of the creatures makes an amazing discovery.

The Little Engine That Could, by Watty Piper (Puffin Books, 1999)
> A little train that carries toys and good things to eat to the children on the other side of the mountain searches for another engine to help get him up the mountain.

Maroo of the Winter Caves, by Ann Turnbull (Clarion Books, 1990)
> After her father is killed, a young girl in the Ice Age must take charge and lead her family to the winter camp. (Chapter Book)

Ming Lo Moves the Mountain, by Arnold Lobel (Mulberry Books, 1993)
> A wise man tells Ming Lo how to move a mountain that is too close to his house.

Moe the Dog in Tropical Paradise, by Diane Stanley (Paper Star, 1999)
> Moe finds a way to beat the winter blues and enjoy island life.

Mommy, Buy Me a China Doll, by Harve Zemach and Margot Zemach (Farrar, Straus & Giroux, 1989)
> A little girl, living in the mountains, suggests a plan to her mother so they can trade for a china doll.

The Mountains of Tibet, by Mordicai Gerstein (Harper Trophy, 1989)
> A Tibetan woodcutter who has always longed to see the world is given the choice of going to heaven or living another life in any part of the world he wishes. His decision surprises even him.

My Little Island, by Frane Lessac (Harper Trophy, 1987)
> A little boy and his best friend go to visit the Caribbean island where the little boy was born.

And My Mean Old Mother Will Be Sorry, Blackboard Bear, by Martha Alexander (Candlewick Press, 2000)
> After a particularly hard day, a little boy decides to run away with his imaginary bear friend and spends the night in a cave before deciding that maybe home is better.

On the Far Side of the Mountain, by Jean Craighead George (E. P. Dutton, 1990)
> Sam's peaceful life is disturbed when his sister runs away from their mountain home and his pet falcon is confiscated. (Chapter Book)

Rosie and the Rustlers, by Roy Gerrard (Sunburst, 1991)
> A poem recounts the adventures of the cowboys on Rosie Jones's ranch, where the mountains meet the prairie.

The Something, by Natalie Babbitt (Farrar, Straus & Giroux, 1987)
> The story of Mylo, who lives in a cave and is afraid of the dark.

The Sun, the Wind and the Rain, by Lisa Westberg Peters (Henry Holt, 1990)
> Gives a side-by-side presentation of the forming of a mountain on Earth and the building of a sand mountain by a young girl, showing how the elements affect both endeavors.

Time of Wonder, by Robert McCloskey (Viking, 1957)
> An island family prepares for the approach of a hurricane and explores the results after the hurricane passes.

A Wave in Her Pocket, by Lynn Joseph (Clarion Books, 1996)
> Five young cousins love to listen to stories told by Tantie, which convey the authentic flavor of Trinidad's folklore. (Chapter Book)

The following books are out of print, but may be available at the local library.

Bayberry Bluff, by Blair Lent (Houghton Mifflin, 1992)
> Tells of the settling of an island off the mainland coast and the people who decide to settle there.

Clyde Monster, by Robert L. Crowe (Puffin Books, 1993)
> Clyde refuses to go to sleep in his cave because he is afraid of the dark.

Summer Business, by Charles E. Martin (Greenwillow Books, 1984)
> Heather and her friends earn money for a trip by starting businesses that cater to the summer visitors to their island.

■ Science Activities

Making a Mountain Out of a Mole Hill

To demonstrate the Earth's movements and the resulting creation of mountains, try this experiment with the students:

- Take several sheets of paper (8 1/2 by 11 inches or larger). Imagine each sheet of paper is a layer of rock.
- Place the papers flat on a tabletop with the left edge of one sheet just touching the right edge of the other sheet. This works best if the longer sides of the papers are touching.
- Holding the outer, long edges of each sheet, push the two pieces of paper toward each other and observe what happens. The two edges that were originally touching each other will rise into a peak as you push the papers.
- This experiment demonstrates the way in which the Earth's movements cause mountains to form when layers of rock are pushed together.

Types of Mountains

There are five basic kinds of mountains: volcanic, fold, fault-block, dome, and erosion. If there are enough students in your class, divide them into five groups and have each group research how one type of mountain was formed. When the research is complete, re-divide the class so that each new group contains some students who have researched different types of mountains. Have the students in these new groups compare and contrast the different types of mountains.

Measuring Mountains

How are mountains measured? Have students research how radar altimeters and laser ranging work. Is one method more accurate than the other? There is now some debate over whether Mt. Everest or Mt. K2 is taller. (They are both mountains in the Himalayan mountain range.)

Locating Mountains

Have students use a globe or an atlas to locate the following mountains:

Mt. Etna (Sicily)

Mt. Everest (Nepal)

Mt. Hood (Oregon)

Mauna Kea (Hawaii)

Mt. Nebo (Jordan)

Mt. Kilimanjaro (Tanzania)

Mt. Olympus (Greece)

Mt. of Olives (E. Jerusalem)

Pike's Peak (Colorado)

Mt. McKinley (Alaska)

Mt. Fuji (Japan)

Mt. Rainier (Washington)

Mt. Rushmore (S. Dakota)

Mt. St. Helens (Washington)

Mt. Matterhorn (Switzerland and Italy)

Mt. Washington (New Hampshire)

Ask the students: Where is the world's longest mountain system, the Mid-Atlantic Range, found (underwater!). What are some islands that are actually peaks of underwater mountains (Iceland, the Azores, Hawaii, the Aleutian Islands)?

Natural Giants

As a class, share the heights of the ten highest mountains and the ten tallest buildings or structures. Have the students prepare a bar graph showing the ten highest mountains, rounding off to the nearest thousand feet. (Each block of your graph can equal 1,000 feet.) Then have them prepare a similar graph showing the tallest man-made structures (skyscrapers, etc.). How do the man-made structures compare in height to the mountains?

Mountain Climbing

Have the students research some of the expeditions that have attempted to climb Mt. Everest. They should answer these questions: How long did it take to scale the mountain? What year was it when the very first group of climbers reached the top? What was the temperature at the top? How many people have died climbing this mountain?

Have the students prepare a list of supplies they would need to bring for an attempt to scale Mt. Everest. They should put together an agenda of what they would accomplish each day, where they would stop for the night, what they would eat, and so forth.

Glaciers

With the students' help, compare and contrast continental glaciers and valley glaciers. Use a Venn Diagram (two circles that overlap—place similarities in the parts that overlap; place differences in the part of the circle that does not overlap) to illustrate similarities and differences between the two.

Locating Glaciers

Where are the glaciers today? Have students locate the following glaciers on a globe or in an atlas:

Mer de Glace (French and Swiss Alps)

Jostedal Glacier (Norway)

Malaspina Glacier (Alaska)

Ross Ice Shelf (Antarctica)

St. Mary's Glacier (Colorado)

Blast from the Past

The city of Pompeii was buried under a 20-foot layer of ash in A.D. 79 when Mt. Vesuvius erupted. Archaeologists have found houses and even a bakery with bread still in the oven there. Have the students research other historical volcanic eruptions. They should include aftereffects of the eruption such as poisonous gas released, starvation due to animals and vegetation being killed, volcanic ash lowering temperatures, and mudflows due to the melting of ice and snow. Following are some volcanic eruptions they may want to investigate:

Mount Laki (Iceland)

Lake Nyos (Cameroon, Africa)

Kilauea (Hawaii)

Nevado del Ruiz (Columbia)

Mount Pinatuba (Philippines)

Mt. St. Helens (Washington)

Volcano in a Bottle (Experiment 1)

Do this experiment with the students:

- You will need 12 inches of string, cold water, a small-necked bottle, warm water, a large glass jar, and red food coloring
- Tie both ends of the string to the neck of the small bottle to make a handle.
- Fill the large jar approximately three-quarters full of cold water. Fill the small bottle with hot water. Add enough red food coloring to the hot water to make the water a bright red.
- Holding the small bottle by the string handle, lower it slowly into the jar of cold water. Be sure to keep the small bottle level as you are lowering it.
- The hot, red water in the small bottle will shoot up into the cold water, resembling a volcano erupting. This happens because the water expands as it is heated and becomes lighter than the cold water in the jar. The hot water rises to the surface because it is lighter.

Volcano in a Bottle (Experiment 2)

Do this experiment with the students:

- You will need one empty 10- or –12-ounce bottle, baking soda, a roasting pan or small tub, vinegar, warm water, a tablespoon, liquid soap, and a measuring cup.
- Place the empty bottle inside the roasting pan or tub. Pour 1 cup of warm water into the bottle.
- Add a few drops of liquid soap to the bottle. Then add 1 tablespoon of baking soda to the soapy water. Suds should rise to the top of the bottle and overflow. If nothing happens, add 1 table-spoon of vinegar to the solution.
- Adding baking soda to warm water starts a chemical reaction and creates carbon dioxide. In the warm water, the carbon dioxide expands, making it lighter than the water and causing it to rise to the top. Similarly, magma inside a volcano erupts because gases expand and force it up and out of the volcano.
- Older students may want to put a plastic bottle in the center of a mound of modeling clay and then mold the clay around the bottle to resemble a mountain. By adding a few drops of red food coloring to the warm water solution, the resulting "eruption" will resemble a real volcano.
- You can also create the necessary chemical reaction by putting 2–3 tablespoons of baking soda into the "volcano" bottle first, then adding a solution consisting of: 1/4 cup vinegar, 1/4 cup water, 1/8 cup liquid detergent, and a few drops of red food coloring.

Watch Out!

To see how destructive a volcano can be, watch *Dante's Peak*. This movie describes many of the warning signals of volcanoes and has scenes that depict the strength of an eruption.

Volcano Pie

Make a volcano pie with your children. Have them help with the measuring and take this opportunity to have a little math lesson along with the fun.

Fudge Sauce (You can also purchase a jar of fudge or
strawberry sauce)
2 ounces unsweetened chocolate
1 cup sugar
1 tablespoon butter
2 tablespoons corn syrup
1/3 cup boiling water
1 teaspoon vanilla

Melt the chocolate and butter over low heat. Add the boiling water and stir well. Add the sugar and corn syrup and bring to a boil. Cover and boil for three minutes. Uncover and cook for two more minutes over reduced heat. Do not stir the mixture while it is cooking. Take the mixture off the heat and add the vanilla.

Crust and Filling
1 prepared chocolate or graham cracker pie crust
1/2 gallon mocha or fudge swirl ice cream
1 cup peanut butter
1 cup chocolate chips

Combine the ice cream (slightly softened) and peanut butter, then mix in the chocolate chips. (Or purchase mocha chip or chocolate/peanut butter ice cream from a local store.) Pile the ice cream into the pie crust, shaping it to look like a volcano. Freeze it for 4 hours or more, until the ice cream is frozen hard. Make a crater in the center of your volcano, then pour the fudge sauce (lava) into it, letting it overflow and run down your mountain. Dust with cocoa and powdered sugar and add any decorations you may have.

Speleothems

Ask the students what speleothems are (cave formations). Speleothems are found in a wide range of colors. Have the students research what causes these differences in color. What minerals can be found in caves? Have them start a notebook of sketches and write descriptions of rimstone, botryiods, cave coral, column, stalactite, stalagmite, flowstone, helectite, and soda straws.

Bats and Caves

Many bats live in caves and, in spite of the darkness, can locate insects to eat. Ask the students how bats "see" in caves (echolocation) and how this method is similar to radar. Have the students look up information on bats and indicate whether the following statements are true or false:

- Bats hang upside down to sleep. (T)
- Most bats carry rabies. (F)
- Bats are mammals that hibernate. (T)
- Bats are blind. (F)
- Bats live in trees, barns, and mines. (T)
- Bats sleep during the day. (T)

Cave Trivia

Following are questions and activities for the students about caves:

- What are troglobites, trogloxenes, and troglophiles? Find three examples of each.
- Where are some of the largest caves located? Look on a map and find the major areas where caves are prominent. Are there more or fewer caves than you thought?
- What is a spelunker? What equipment would you want to have with you if you were going spelunking? Do some research on exactly how spelunking is done. Make a list of the items you think a spelunker should carry in a backpack.

Stalagmites and Stalactites

Create your own stalagmites and stalactites as a class:

- Fill two glass jars (quart size) with hot water. Stir 4 ounces alum into each jar.
- Take a piece of yarn (about 2 feet long) and tie a small rock onto each end. Then tie a loop in the middle of the piece of yarn (do not make a knot, just a loop in the yarn). Place one of the rocks into each jar of water. Let the loop hang down between the two jars (it should hang 2 to 3 inches above the table).
- Let this apparatus sit, undisturbed, for two or three days. Then watch as a stalactite forms on the yarn and a stalagmite forms on the table.

Island Paradises

Ask the students to locate several islands on a world map (e.g., Australia, the Falkland Islands, Hawaiian Islands, Cuba, Greenland, Easter Island, the Canary Islands, Midway Island, Iceland, Tahiti, Puerto Rico, the Aleutian Islands, Greece, Sicily). Are all islands tropical paradises, warm and covered with palm trees? Have students choose several islands and do the following:

- Graph the average temperature of the islands.
- Chart the square footage of the islands.
- Compare and contrast the plant and animal life. Does the type of plant and animal life that exists on each island affect what the natives eat and how they live?
- Investigate local customs and beliefs. Are these customs and beliefs consistent with the location of the islands on the world map? If not, how would you explain this difference?

Making a Relief Map

As a class, make a relief map. You'll need:

```
3 cups flour
glue
1 cup salt
a pencil
3 tablespoons dry wheat paste powder
a small saucepan
1 1/4 cups lukewarm water
paintbrushes
large piece of thick cardboard
a wooden spoon
a large piece of white construction paper
    (same size as cardboard)
craft paints
a large mixing bowl
an atlas or encyclopedia
```

This recipe can be used when making any topographical map.

- Draw the outline of the map you are making on the white construction paper. Glue the paper to the cardboard.
- To make the dough, heat the salt in the pan over low heat for about 5 minutes. Mix the salt, flour, and paste together in the mixing bowl. Add the lukewarm water slowly, stirring continuously. If your mixture seems too dry, add additional water, a little at a time. Knead the dough until it is soft and pliable.
- Use chunks of dough to fill in your map. Do the highest points of elevation first (refer to the map in the atlas or encyclopedia). Fill in the rest of your map with dough, arranging it to fit your outline. Let it dry.
- Paint on the details you want to show on your map after it is completely dry. Use smaller paintbrushes for detail work and larger ones for area work.

Scientific Theory

To discover why some scientists believe that all the continents were one supercontinent called Pangaea, try this with your class:

- You'll need: a map of the world, thin cardboard, tracing paper, pencil, glue, and scissors.
- Trace over the outline of each continent by placing your tracing paper over the world map.
- Glue your tracing onto the cardboard and cut out each continent.
- Try fitting the continents together like a jigsaw puzzle. Do you think that they fit together well? (Scientists explain that the continents do not fit together perfectly because the edges of each continent are underwater.)

Earthquakes

As a class, research and discuss several earthquakes, their locations, and the extent of the damage they have caused. Ask the students to contemplate what, if anything, could have been done prior to these natural disasters to lessen the amount of damage and loss of life. What steps are being taken to reduce damage from future earthquakes? Students can create posters that illustrate safety precautions to be taken during an earthquake.

■ Creative Writing Activities

Following are instructions to give the students for various writing activities.

- Make up an imaginary animal friend to play with. What kind of animal would it be? What would it look like? What activities would you do together? Write a story about one particular adventure that you and your imaginary friend have. (*And My Mean Old Mother Will Be Sorry, Blackboard Bear* by Alexander)

- Do you have something that you are afraid of, or dislike, but don't want others to know about? Write an entry for your personal journal that tells about your fear. Try to think of ways in which you can overcome it. (*The Something* by Babbitt)

- Think of things that scare you. Turn the tables and pretend that you scare the things you fear! Write a funny story about this situation. (*Clyde Monster* by Crowe)

- If you could live anywhere in the world, where would it be? What type of life would you live? Why? Write a letter to a friend in which you answer these questions. (*The Mountains of Tibet* by Gerstein)

- Pretend that you have gone on a hiking or camping trip into the mountains with your friends. You decide to spend the night in a cave that you discover in the side of one of the mountains. The inside of the cave has pictures painted on it that seem to tell a story of people from days gone by. You and your friends try to figure out what the pictures say. Draw the pictures you have found in the cave. Write the story they tell. (*Blaze and the Indian Cave* by Anderson)

- What is meant by "no man is an island"? Reflect on the ways that you depend on others and write a story about a situation in which you are glad to have someone around when you need help.

- When someone behaves as though a small problem or inconvenience is a major concern, that person is said to be "making a mountain out of a molehill." Can you remember any time when you (or a friend) may have been guilty of making a mountain out of a molehill? Write your version of the incident, including the reasons why the problem was really not as severe as you made it out to be.

- Throughout the history of the United States, there have been several incidents of severe earthquakes occurring in California. Read some of the newspaper and magazine articles about these disasters. Then write a story describing what you think you would experience and feel if an earthquake hit your city. (*Earthquake 2099* by Sullivan) As a follow-up for this activity, compile a list of safety rules to be followed during an earthquake

- Pretend that you live on an island. One day when you are walking along the beach you find something that has been washed ashore. What did you find? Write a story that tells either the tale of how the item you found came to be on your island or what happens to you and the item after you recover it. (*Sarah's Bear* by Koci)

- You are vacationing on a tropical island when a volcano that has been inactive for years suddenly comes to life and threatens the village where you are staying. Write a story describing your adventures on this volcanic isle.

- You have joined a group of adventurers who plan to spend their vacation participating in a survival test. The group will take minimal supplies to a tropical island and fend for themselves for a period of two weeks. Keep a journal that describes your preparations for this trip and your daily activities after arriving on the island. (*Island of the Blue Dolphins* by O'Dell)

■ Art Activities

Following are instructions to give the students for various art activities.

- Draw a picture of your favorite baby animals playing in their natural habitat. Be sure to make the surroundings as authentic as possible. (*Watching Foxes* by Arnosky)

- Make a picture story showing how two enemies put aside their differences and work together so that both benefit. Be sure to do your entire story in pictures only. (*The Knight and the Dragon* by de Paola)

- Make an island out of salt dough.

> 2 cups flour
> 1 cup salt
> 1 cup water
>
> Mix the flour, salt, and water together. Use a sturdy piece of cardboard (or wood), painted blue, for your base. Form an island out of the dough mixture. Form mountain ranges, valleys, lakes, and rivers out of the dough. Let the dough dry thoroughly. Paint your island paradise with watercolors, tempera paints, or markers.

- Make a volcano out of play dough.

> 1 cup flour
> 1/2 cup salt
> 2 tablespoons cream of tartar
> 1/2 cup water
> 2 teaspoons food coloring
> 1 tablespoon cooking oil
>
> In a medium-sized pot, mix the first three ingredients. Then add the rest of the ingredients. Cook over medium heat 3–5 minutes. After your dough has cooled, place it on a piece of sturdy cardboard or a piece of wood. Shape the dough to look like a volcano. (Use reference books listed in "Teaching Resources" for models.) Paint your volcano, making the tip of the volcano and lines running down the sides red to resemble lava flow. You can also use modeling clay that hardens to make your volcano. This can be purchased in art and hobby stores.

- Make a bear hiding in a cave. Cut out two identical mountains or hills, 6 to 8 inches high and 6 to 8 inches wide. Use gray or manila-colored paper. In one of the mountains, cut out an opening for a cave (about 3 inches high). Staple or tape the two mountains together, leaving a 4-inch opening on one side. Using brown construction paper, cut out a bear figure about 2 inches tall. Cut a strip of cardboard (about 2 by 8 inches) and attach it to the back of the bear. Insert the cardboard strip through the opening in the side of the mountain. Now your bear can hide in the cave and appear when he wants to. (*Beady Bear* by Freeman)

- Make a cave lantern. You will need one piece of black construction paper (9 by 12 inches) and one piece of yellow construction paper that has been trimmed to 8 by 11 inches. Fold the black construction paper lengthwise. Make several cuts through the folded side of the paper. The cuts should be placed 1 inch apart and should stop 1 inch from the open edge of the paper. Make a tube out of the yellow paper. The tube will be 8 inches tall. Staple or tape the tube together. Wrap the black paper tightly around the yellow tube so that the folded slits point outward. Tape or staple the black paper to the yellow tube. The yellow paper will now peek through the slits in the black paper, resembling light. Cut a 1-inch-wide strip of black paper (about 12 inches long) and attach the ends to each side of the top of the lantern as a handle. You can also cut shapes and designs in the black paper instead of the slits. You will have an attractive lantern.

- With the rest of the class, sing songs about the mountains and valleys, such as:

  "She'll Be Coming 'round The Mountain"

  "Down in the Valley"

  "Rocky Mountain High"

  "Go Tell It on the Mountain"

- Read *High in the Mountains* by Radin. Create your own depiction of a scene familiar to you, using colors as the main means of getting across the feel of the place you are showing.

- Have a tropical island party (*My Little Island* by Lessac). Listen to Hawaiian, calypso, or steel drum music. Have a snack of different tropical fruits. Experiment with the hula hoop and have a limbo contest. Try island dances.

  Make leis by cutting flower shapes out of tissue paper or construction paper. Poke two holes in the center of each single flower and construct a flower by putting three or four single flowers together using pipe cleaners, needle and thread, or ribbon fed through the center holes. Tie the flowers together on a piece of strong thread or string to make your necklace. You can also make a lei to wear on your head.

  Make hula skirts using green tissue paper and construction paper. Make the waist of the skirt by cutting long strips of construction paper (4 inches wide and the length of your piece of construction paper). Tape the strips together until they are long enough to go around your waist. Fold this strip in half (so it is 2 inches wide), then cut 1/2-inch-wide strips of tissue paper, the length that you want your skirt to be. Glue or staple these strips to your waistband (place each strip inside the fold to give your skirt a finished look). You can make a skirt that goes all the way around or just have strips hanging down in the front.

- Make a tropical island scene. Cut out sandpaper in whatever form you want your island to be. Glue the island onto blue construction paper to serve as your water. Make trees, underbrush, huts, and so forth, out of construction paper, toothpicks, Popsicle sticks, tissue paper, or whatever you can find. Make some natives out of cardboard and dress them by gluing on small scraps of paper for clothes. (*The Empty Island* by Smith)

- Draw a picture showing what you would consider the perfect island paradise to be. What type of and how many people would live there? What foods would you eat? Where would you live? What activities would you participate in (*The Jolly Mon* by Buffett and Buffett)? (Older students can make this a 3-dimensional picture by making mountains, trees, people, etc., out of construction paper or clay.)

- Make a mountain out of a brown lunchbag. Stuff the lunchbag three-quarters full with crumpled newspaper. Be sure that the lunchbag is well stuffed. Tie the top of the lunchbag (directly above the stuffing) together with a string (or use a rubberband). There should be about 2 1/2 to 3 inches of bag protruding above the string. Turn the top of the lunchbag down over the string (hiding it). Paint this top part white to resemble snow on the top of a mountain. You can paint the bottom of the mountain or leave it as it is. (*The Sun, the Wind and the Rain* by Peters)

Additional Resources

■ Experiment Books

Backyard Scientist, It's Like Magic Super Crystal Kit, by Jane Hoffman (self-published, 1992)
>Activities teach children to use the scientific method to observe, question, and hypothesize while exploring the world of crystals.

Discover Rocks and Minerals, by Laura C. Beattie (Carnegie Museum of Natural History, 1994)
>Contains experiments involving rocks and minerals.

Earth Science for Every Kid, by Janice Van Cleave (John Wiley & Sons, 1991)
>Instructions for experiments, each of which introduces an earth science concept. Includes experiments on rocks and minerals, crystal movement, erosion, atmosphere, weather, and oceans.

Geology Projects for Young Scientists, by Bruce Smith and David McKay (Econo-Clad, 1999)
>Experiments and projects explore the Earth's age, plate tectonics, earthquakes, and crystals.

How the Earth Works, by John Farndon (Reader's Digest, 1992)
>Contains brief descriptions and many experiments on exploring the Earth's structure, features, and changing conditions.

■ *National Geographic* Articles

Bodies of Freshwater

1993 Special Edition—"Water—The Power, Promise and Turmoil of North America's Fresh Water"

January 1994—"Great Flood of '93," page 42

December 1993—"The Superior Way of Life," page 70

September 1993—"The Pecos, River of Hard-Won Dreams," page 38

August 1993—"Untamed Treasure of the Cumberland," page 123

June 1993—"Bangladesh: When the Water Comes," page 118

February 1993—"Mekong River," page 2

September 1992—"Minnesota Memoir," page 92

August 1992—"Main-Danube Canal Links Europe's Waterways," page 3

July 1992—"America's Third Coast," page 2

June 1992—"The World's Great Lake," page 2; "Bikini's Nuclear Graveyard," page 70

April 1992—"Blackwater Country," page 34

November 1991—"Lifeline for a Nation—Zaire River," page 5

July 1991—"Docklands—London's New Frontier," page 32

The Ocean

December 1991—"Australia's Magnificent Pearls," page 109

February 1991—"Allies in the Deep," page 39

Landforms

April 1993—"Mauritius, Island of Quiet Success," page 110

February 1993—"In the Heart of Appalachia," page 112

December 1992—"Volcanoes: Crucibles of Creation," page 5; "Gatekeepers of the Himalayas," page 70

November 1992—"The Lure of the Catskills," page 108

July 1992—"The Spell of the Trobriand Islands," page 117

June 1992—"Cuttyhunk Seasons," page 114

October 1991—"Lord Howe Island," page 126

May 1991—"Bhutan, Kingdom in the Clouds," page 79

March 1991—"The Splendors of Lechuguilla Cave," page 34

■ Magazine Articles

"Kids Discover," *Volcanoes* (June/July 1993)

■ Organizations

The Ocean

Marine Education Project
Pacific Science Center
200 Second Ave., North
Seattle, WA 98109
ocean-related curriculum activities,
grade specific

Marine Information Service
Sea Grant College Program
Texas A&M University
College Station, TX 77843
Sea Sources, children's literature about the sea

Oceanic Society
218 D St., SE
Washington, D.C. 20003

Office of Coastal Zone Management
National Oceanic and Atmospheric
Administration
3300 Whitehaven St., NW
Washington, D.C. 20235
Coastal Awareness, resource guide for
elementary school teachers

Office of Coastal Zone Management
National Oceanic and Atmospheric
Administration
3300 Whitehaven St., NW
Washington, D.C. 20235
Coastal Awareness, resource guide for
elementary school teachers

UNC Sea Grant
105 1911 Building
N. Carolina State University
Raleigh, NC 27650
several experiment and activity guides

U. S. Department of Commerce
National Oceanic & Atmospheric Administration
National Ocean Survey
Rockville, MD 20852

U. S. Department of Commerce, NOAA
Coastal Zone Information Center
Washington, D.C. 20235
Coastal Awareness Resource Guide,
grade specific

Landforms

American Cave Conservation
P.O. Box 409
Horse Cave, KY 42749

National Speleological Society
Cave Ave.
Huntsville, AL 35810

American Coal Foundation
1130 17th St., NW Suite 220
Washington, D.C. 20036

Soil Conservation Service
P.O. Box 2890
Washington, D.C. 20013

National Cave Association
Route 9, P.O. Box 106
McMinnville, TX 37110

U.S. Department of Energy
Office of Education, Business & Labor Affairs
613 G St., NW
Washington, DC 20037

National Coal Association
Educational Division
1130 17th St., NW
Washington, D.C. 20036

USDA-SCS
Room 0054-S
P.O. Box 2890
Washington, D.C. 20013
soil erosion by water packet

Water

The American Ground Water Trust
6375 Riverside Dr.
Dublin, OH 43017
(614) 761-2215
"Ground Water Education in America's Schools"

National Arbor Day Foundation
100 Arbor Ave.
Nebraska City, NE 68410
incorporates water into the study of trees

Classroom GEMS SEE-North
University of Michigan Biological Station
Pellston, MI 49769
set of lesson plans on water

Wisconsin Natural Resources
P. O. Box 7191
Madison, WI 53707-7191
workbook on protecting groundwater

Climate Institute
316 Pennsylvania Ave., SE
Washington, D.C. 20036
statistical data on water

USGS, Branch of Distribution
P.O. Box 25286
Denver Federal Center
Denver, CO 80225
wetlands poster

Michigan Geographic Alliance
c/o Joe Stoltman
Department of Geography
Western Michigan University
Kalamazoo, MI 49008
information on the Great Lakes

Geology

American Geological Institute
4220 King St.
Alexandria, VA 22302

U.S. Geological Survey
Geological Inquiries Group
907 National Center
Reston, VA 22092
pamphlets, books, maps

Carolina Biological Supply Co.
2700 York Rd.
Burlington, NC 27215
rock/mineral samples, fossils, geology
materials

Ward's Natural Science Establishment
5100 West Henrietta Rd.
P.O. Box 92912
Rochester, NY 14692-9012
rock/mineral samples, fossils

Delta Education
P.O. Box 915
Hudson, NH 03051
rock/mineral samples, crystal-growing kits,
charts, guides

■ Videos/Films

Britannica Films & Video
310 S. Michigan Ave.
Chicago, IL 60604
geology films

PBS VIDEO
1320 Braddock Place
Alexandria, VA 22314
fourteen 28-minute geology videos,
upper level

Coronet Film & Video
108 Wilmot Rd.
Deerfield, IL 60015
geology films

Society for Visual Education
Dept. BJ
1345 Diversey Pkwy.

Karol Media
350 N. Pennsylvania Ave.
Wilkes-Barre, PA 18773
Earth: The Restless Planet, film or video,
upper level

Society for Visual Education
Dept. BJ
1345 Diversey Pkwy.
Chicago, IL 60614-1299
Introducing Geology (grade 3+), set of six
filmstrips with cassettes

■ Software

Educational Activities
P.O. Box 392
Freeport, NY 11520
Earth: The Inside Story (grades 3+);
The Earth Through Time and Space (grades 5+);
available for Apple II computers

■ Web Sites

The following Web sites will reference additional Web sites relating to the Earth. These sites were accessed in March 2001 and were active at that time.

Caves:
> http://cavern.com
> http://www.surfnetkids.com/caves.htm

Earthquakes:
> http://earthquake.usgs.gov/4kids/

Glaciers:
> http://www.surfnetkids.com/glacier
> http://www.nps.gov/olym/edglac.htm

Oceans:
> http://www.microsoft.com/kids/msb/ocean.htm
> http:www.epa.gov/owow/oceans/kids/html

Plate Tectonics:
> http://sciencespot.net/pages/kdzethsi.html
> http://www.ajkids.com/tours/earthquaketour.asp

Rocks and Minerals:
> http://www.ghgcorp.com/gpenning/index.htm
> http://www.gemandmineral.com/states/html

Volcanoes:
> http://vulcan.wr.usgs.gov/volcanoes/framework.html
> http://www.learner.org/exhibits/volcanoes/entry.html

ECOLOGY

- Key Concepts

- Comprehensive Teaching Resources

- Chapter 1: Endangered Animals

- Chapter 2: Diminishing Resources

- Chapter 3: Pollution

- Additional Resources

Key Concepts

■ Primary Concepts

Students will be able to:

1. Understand that some animals are endangered. (Chapter 1).

2. Understand that some resources are decreasing and that humans cannot re-create them (Chapter 2).

3. Explain that polluted water and air can be harmful to our environment (Chapter 3).

4. Recognize the negative effect that littering has on the environment (Chapter 3).

5. Recognize that everyone has the responsibility of helping to keep the Earth clean (Chapter 3).

    Know the meaning of *biodegradable* and *recycle.*

6. Understand the necessity of recycling paper, aluminum, and plastic products and realize the negative impact of improper disposal of these items (Chapter 3).

7. Recognize the negative impact of improper disposal of Styrofoam products (Chapter 3).

■ Intermediate Concepts

Students will be able to:

1. List various endangered animals (Chapter 1).

2. Hypothesize about why these animals may have become endangered (Chapter 1).

3. Describe ways of protecting wild animals (Chapter 1).

4. Hypothesize what might happen if wild animals (endangered and others) were not protected (Chapter 1).

5. Describe the interdependence of life (Chapter 1).

6. Name the natural resources that are in danger (air, water, trees, land) and discuss reasons why (Chapter 2).

7. Demonstrate an understanding of the importance of environmental issues in our daily lives (Chapters 2, 3).

    Understand the following terms: *biodegradable, recycle, landfill, environment, synthetics, greenhouse effect.*

    Understand the part that man-made materials (such as synthetics and plastics) play in our environment and their practical uses in our daily lives.

8. Participate in Earth Day conservation and recycling projects and activities during April (Chapters 2, 3).

9. Apply conservation practices to their daily habits (Chapters 2, 3).

10. Understand the following facts about air: (Chapters 2, 3).

    Air has pressure and this pressure helps you breathe.

    Warm air rises and cold air sinks because cold air is heavier than warm air.

    Air is made up of nitrogen, oxygen, carbon dioxide, and water vapor.

    More carbon dioxide in the air decreases the amount of oxygen.

11. Describe the oxygen cycle (Chapters 2, 3).

12. Cite examples of the positive impact that technology has had on our environment (Chapters 1, 2, 3):

    catalytic converters, unleaded gasoline, air filters on cars, and scrubbers in smokestacks of factories

    cleaning of our water supply

    protecting endangered animals

13. Cite examples of the harmful effects that modern technology has had on our environment, including wildlife and human beings (Chapters 1, 2, 3).

14. Understand that when something interferes with the oxygen cycle, air pollution is produced (Chapters 2, 3).

15. Discuss pollutants and their dangers and describe conservation strategies in use (Chapters 2, 3).

16. Name the sources of fresh water (lake water, pond water, river water, groundwater—rain, melted snow, and ice) and the three main sources of pollution of this water supply (pesticides, fertilizers, and laundry detergent) (Chapters 2, 3). Understand the harmful effects of water pollution on all living things.

17. Build an awareness of the negative effects of man-made materials on our environment (Chapter 3).

18. Participate in hands-on activities that demonstrate the effect of pollution and how people can clean up the environment to negate some of these effects (Chapter 3).

19. Document the harmful effects of waste in our environment, then name ways that they, as individuals, can have a positive impact on minimizing these effects (Chapter 3).

20. Understand that the ozone layer screens out the harmful ultraviolet rays of the sun (Chapter 3).

21. Differentiate between biodegradable and non-biodegradable materials (Chapter 3).

22. Understand how landfills are used to reduce land pollution and the importance of using biodegradable materials (Chapter 3).

23. Name the two main sources of chemical wastes in the Earth's soil (pesticides and chemical wastes in landfills) (Chapter 3).

24. Cite sources of ocean pollution, discussing the effects of oil spills and means of effectively cleaning up these spills (Chapter 3).

25. Discuss the process that occurs at a water treatment plant (Chapter 3).

■ Upper Concepts

Students will be able to:

1. Describe the formation and uses of fossil fuels (Chapter 2).

2. Differentiate between renewable and non-renewable resources (Chapter 2).

3. Cite examples of how to conserve fossil fuels (Chapter 2).

4. Understand that certain materials absorb solar energy better than others (Chapter 2).

5. Explain the negative environmental and economic effects associated with using fossil fuels as an energy resource (Chapters 2, 3).

6. Discuss how air can be conserved and cite reasons why it should be conserved (Chapter 2).

7. Cite examples of energy alternatives to fossil fuels (wind, water, geothermal, nuclear, and solar), and compare advantages and disadvantages of each (Chapters 2, 3).

8. Explain the harmful effects of acid rain (Chapter 3).

Comprehensive Teaching Resources

The following table lists books that cover a wide range of topics about ecology. One of these books could serve as your main teaching guide while studying this unit. Each book is listed with a short summary, and the chapters in this book that it applies to are noted. The books are listed by degree of difficulty, easiest to most difficult.

BOOK AND SUMMARY	AUTHOR	CHAPTERS		
		1	2	3
How Green Are You? (Clarkson Potter, 1991) Using fun-filled activities and illustrations, gives information on how we can help save energy, protect wildlife, and avoid pollution.	David Bellamy	X	X	X
Earth Day (First Avenue Editions, 1992) Discusses Earth Day 1970 and 1990, with their accompanying activities that called attention to pollution, environmental destruction, and waste of natural resources.	Linda Lowery		X	X
Every Kid's Guide to Saving the Earth (Ideal Children's Books, 1993) Comic-like illustrations show how children can show concern for their planet by conserving resources, reducing pollution, and preserving nature.	Joy Berry	X	X	X
Ecology (Dorling Kindersley, 2000) Brief text and excellent illustrations describe all aspects of ecology.	Steve Pollock	X	X	X
Environmental America, the North Central States (Millbrook Press, 1991) One of a series of books that looks at the impact of humans and society on the environment. Each book covers a particular area of the United States.	D. J. Herda	X	X	X
Saving Planet Earth (Franklin Watts, 1992) Concise text describes the advantages and drawbacks of various plans to save and protect the Earth's resources, wilderness areas, plants, animals, and tribal peoples.	Rosalind Kerven	X	X	X
Earth Book for Kids (Learning Works, 1990) Facts and statistics on environmental issues include rain forest destruction, recycling, and endangered animals. Includes games, crafts, and ideas for activities.	Linda Schwartz	X	X	X
Atlas of Environmental Issues (Facts on File, 1989) Describes and explains some environmental issues such as soil erosion, deforestation, oil pollution, acid rain, noise, and endangered species.	Dr. Nick Middleton	X	X	X

Each chapter in this section lists reference books that focus on the specific area of ecology being addressed. These books can be used to complement and expand upon the basic information provided in the comprehensive resource books listed in the table above.

The reference books in each chapter have been classified by age level to help you select those that best fit the needs and interests of your student(s).

Chapter 1
Endangered Animals

■ Teaching Resources

Books containing experiment(s) relating to the subject matter are marked with a plus sign (+) before and after the title.

P   *Animals in Danger,* by Janine Amos (Raintree Steck-Vaughn, 1992)
Simplistic text and numerous color illustrations and photos explore the problems of endangered animals and what is being done to protect them.

P   *Caring for Our Animals,* by Carol Greene (Enslow, 1991)
Simple text and black-and-white illustrations explain animal issues such as habitat destruction, the fur trade, and wild animal pets, along with activities you can do to protect animals.

P   *Endangered Animals,* by Lynn M. Stone (Children's Press, 1984)
Easy-to-read text describes various endangered animals throughout the world, why and how they became endangered, and what can be done to save them.

P   *The Picnic,* by Chris Baines and Penny Ives (Interlink, 1990)
One of four books (*The Old Boot, The Flower,* and *The Nest*) that introduce children to nature and the environment. This book explains what happens to a children's picnic, with cute illustrations.

P   *Where Are My Prairie Dogs and Black-Footed Ferrets?,* by Ron Hirschi (Bantam Books, 1992)
Uses exceptional photos, with brief text, to describe prairie dog and ferret habitats, grassland destruction and its consequences, and ways we can save the animals.

P   *Where Are My Swans, Whooping Cranes, and Singing Loons?,* by Ron Hirschi (Bantam Books, 1992)
Exceptional photographs and brief text are used to describe the lifestyles of the swan, whooping crane, and loon and destruction of the wetlands and how it affects their survival.

P/I *Children's Guide to Endangered Animals,* by Roger Few (Macmillan, 1993)
Information on endangered species throughout the world, what is threatening their survival, and what is being done to save them. Concise text and nice illustrations make for a good resource book.

P/I *Saving the Peregrine Falcon,* by Caroline Arnold (Lerner, 1990)
Santa Cruz Predatory Bird Research Group's work to save the peregrine falcon from extinction is discussed.

P/I *Will We Miss Them? Endangered Species,* by Alexandra Wright (Econo-Clad, 1999)
Written by a sixth-grader, each double-page spread introduces a different endangered animal and includes an explanation of why it is in jeopardy.

P/I/U   *Earthwise at Play,* by Linda Lowery and Marybeth Lorbiecki (Carolrhoda Books, 1993)
Introduces endangered species and habitats, ecological concepts, and how we can enjoy and save wildlife.

P/I/U   *Endangered Animals—Zoo Books,* by John Bonnett Wexo (Creative Education), 1988
Excellent pictures and informative text, in a magazine format, about endangered animals, where they are located, and what's being done to protect them.

I   *Animals in Danger,* by Janine Amos (Raintree Steck-Vaughn, 1993)
Describes the problems of endangered animals and the work being done to save them.

I   *Big Cats,* by Seymour Simon (Harper Trophy, 1994)
Habitats and habits of tigers, snow leopards, cheetahs, and lions are described through colorful pictures.

I   *Endangered Forest Animals,* by Dave Taylor (Crabtree, 1992)
Contains a brief description of the forest, followed by two-page descriptions of a number of endangered animals that live there. Part of a series that includes *Endangered Grassland Animals, Endangered Mountain Animals,* and *Endangered Wetland Animals.*

I   *Places of Refuge, Our National Wildlife Refuge System,* by Dorothy Hinshaw Patent (Clarion Books, 1992)
Beautiful photographs and concise text describe the refuges in Texas, North Dakota, and California, with focus on the different methods of maintaining nature's balance.

I   *Wolves,* by R. D. Lawrence (Sierra Club Juvenile Books, 1994)
Explains the life cycle of wolves and how they interact.

I/U *The Atlas of Endangered Animals,* by Steve Pollock (Facts on File, 1993)
Describes the endangered species of animals throughout the world, through text and helpful maps.

I/U *Discover Rain Forests,* by Lynne Hardie Baptista (Publications International, 1993)
Concise explanation of rain forests and their inhabitants. It is a good resource, with a glossary.

I/U *Endangered Species,* by Christopher Lampton and Karen Vergoth (Franklin Watts, 1999)
Explains why some species are threatened and how others become extinct. It includes a thorough list of endangered and threatened wildlife throughout the world.

I/U *Endangered Species: Our Endangered Planet,* by Sunni Bloyd (Lucent, 1989)
Extinct and endangered animals are discussed, with special emphasis on the ferret, tiger, and condor. A glossary and a listing of organizations active in protecting wildlife are included.

I/U *Gorilla Rescue,* by Jill Bailey (Steck-Vaughn, 1990)
Puts fictional characters in factual situations to explain the reasons for the declining gorilla population.

I/U *Kids Can Save the Animals! 101 Easy Things to Do,* by Ingrid Newkirk (Warner Books, 1991)
Information on the ways in which children can help animals, ease their living conditions, and promote their proper treatment.

I/U *Manatee: On Location,* by Kathy Darling (Lothrop, Lee & Shepard, 1991)
Full-page, color photographs help describe the life of Florida's manatees.

I/U *Saving Endangered Animals,* by Virginia Silverstein, Alvin Silverstein, and Robert Silverstein (Enslow, 1993)
Current efforts to prevent endangerment and extinction of different species of wildlife are explored, in clear text and black-and-white photos.

I/U *Towns and Cities,* by Rodney Aldis (Dillon, 1992)
Examines urban plants and animals, their survival techniques in the city, and methods of keeping them from becoming endangered. Other books in the series are *Seas and Oceans, Rainforests, Polar Lands, Deserts, Grasslands, Rivers, Ponds and Lakes,* and *Mountains.*

I/U *And Then There Was One: The Mysteries of Extinction,* by Margery Facklam (Little, Brown, 1993)
Describes how breeding programs and legislatures have helped some near-extinct animals. It includes numerous illustrations.

I/U *Walrus: On Location,* by Kathy Darling (Lothrop, Lee & Shepard, 1991)
Walrus life is examined. Contains excellent photographs and includes ideas for conservation.

■ Reading Selections

Books marked with an asterisk (*) before and after the title are related to activities in the activity sections of this chapter.

Aardvarks, Disembark!, by Ann Jonas (Puffin Books, 1994)
After the Flood, Noah discovers many unfamiliar animals as the creatures disembark. Then, as he journeys down the mountain, he encounters species that are now extinct or endangered.

Baaa, by David Macaulay (Houghton Mifflin, 1985)
After humans disappear from Earth, sheep take over. They make the same mistakes and eventually disappear as well. (Chapter Book)

A Beach for the Birds, by Bruce McMillan (Houghton Mifflin, 1993)
The author takes the reader on a tour of a beach in Maine that is a wildlife refuge for families of rare birds.

Dear Mr. Blueberry, by Simon James (Econo-Clad, 1999)
Emily writes to her teacher asking for advice when she believes she has seen a whale in her pond.

The Empty Island, by Roger Smith (Interlink, 1991)
A man and his family live in harmony with the animals on an island until the man and his wife decide they would like to have the animals' clothes for themselves.

The Gnats of Knotty Pine, by Bill Peet (Houghton Mifflin), 1984
The creatures of Knotty Pine Forest meet every year on the eve of the first day of hunting season to try to think of ways to save themselves.

The Great Kapok Tree, by Lynne Cherry (Harcourt Brace Jovanovich, 1990)
> The many different animals that live in a great Kapok tree in the Brazilian rain forest try to convince a man with an ax not to cut down their home.

Hey! Get Off Our Train, by John Burningham (Crown, 1999)
> A young boy takes a trip on his toy train and saves several endangered animals.

Humphrey the Lost Whale, by Wendy Tokuda (Econo-Clad, 1999)
> The true story of how people around the San Francisco area helped save a beached whale.

Hunter and the Animals, by Tomie de Paola (Holiday House, 1988)
> Forest animals play a trick on a sleeping hunter. (Wordless Book)

Jenny's Corner, by Frederic Bell (Sunburst, 1995)
> Jenny's love of deer results in hunting being prohibited in her valley. (Chapter Book)

Racso and the Rats of Nimh, by Jane Conly (Harper & Row, 1986)
> Timothy and Racso try to prevent the destruction of a community of rats who can read and write. (Chapter Book)

Sally and the Limpet, by Simon James (Margaret K. McElderry, 1991)
> Sally gets a limpet stuck to her finger while at the beach.

Secret of the Seal, by Deborah Davis (Random House Children's Books, 1994)
> Kyo, an Eskimo boy, must make a difficult choice between his family loyalty and his friendship with a seal. (Chapter Book)

The Turtle Watchers, by Pamela Powell (Puffin Books, 1994)
> Three sisters on an island work together to save leatherback turtles from poachers. (Chapter Book)

The Year of the Panda, by Miriam Schlein (Harper Trophy, 1992)
> A Chinese boy learns why pandas are endangered after rescuing a baby panda from starvation. (Chapter Book)

The following books are out of print, but may be available at the local library.

Aldita and the Forest, by Thelma Catterwell (Houghton Mifflin, 1989)
> A newly born butterly, the last of her kind, helps many other forest creatures and is rewarded by being turned into a butterfly orchid.

Chimpanzee Kid, by Ron Roy (Clarion Books, 1985)
> Harold, interested in animal rights, is joined by a new boy in class in an effort to free a caged laboratory chimp. (Chapter Book)

Danger on the Arctic Ice, by Elizabeth Sackett (Little, Brown, 1991)
> As summer approaches, a small harp seal encounters danger from hunters and animals alike (Chapter Book)

Donald and the Fish that Walked, by Edward Ricciuti (Harper & Row, 1974)
> The walking catfish, which had been brought to Florida as an addition to an aquarium, soon spread and threaten the ecological balance.

The Grizzly Sisters, by Cathy Bellows (Macmillan, 1991)
> The Grizzly sisters live to regret it when they disobey their mom's warning to stay away from tourists.

Henry's Wrong Turn, by Harriet Ziefert and Andrea Baruffi (Little, Brown, 1989)
A humpback whale gets lost and ends up in New York Harbor. Based on a true story.

IBIS: A True Whale Story, by John Himmelman (Scholastic, 1991)
Tells the storyof a humpback whale calf who gets tangled in a fishing net.

Lion on the Mountain, by Paige Dixon (Atheneum, 1992)
A young boy suspects that a guest who joins him and his father on their trip is more interesting in killing the animals than in photographing them. (Chapter Book)

The Old Ladies Who Liked Cats, by Carol Greene (HarperCollins, 1991)
An island's ecology is disturbed when the old ladies are no longer allowed to let their cats out at night.

A Wolf Story, by David McPhail (Charles Scribner's Sons, 1981)
A wolf is captured to be used in a film. He escapes and is about to be killed when a group of children befriend him.

■ Science Activities

Protecting Endangered Animals

Have a class discussion about what would be the best ways to help protect animals that are now endangered. Make a list of the students' suggestions. Call or write your local zoo for information on endangered animals and organizations or programs that exist to try to preserve these species. As a class, put together a flyer that tells about the animals' plight and presents information on ways to help. Distribute your flyer to students' parents or around your neighborhood to try to solicit help.

Animal Time Line

Choose several extinct animals to study, or divide the class into groups and have each group choose an extinct animal to research. Make a time line of the animals being studied, listing the last sighting of each species. To prepare such a time line, students will need to find specific information about each species and/or make judgments about what caused each species' extinction.

Profile of the Endangered Animal

Share the following information with the students. Animals are more apt to become extinct if they
interfere in some way with people's activities,

migrate,

have very specific food or nesting requirements,

are very sensitive to change, or

have a small number of offspring and a long gestation period.

As a class, make a list of endangered species. Divide into cooperative groups (or choose two or three species to research) and rank each of the species according to the criteria listed above. This will involve in-depth research to substantiate each classification.

Where Are They?

Chart the location of different endangered species on a world map. Have each child pick an endangered species and write an informational booklet about it. The booklet should include the country or habitat the animal comes from, the animal's physical characteristics, what it eats, why it is becoming extinct, how many of the species are left, and efforts being taken to protect the species. Have the children make durable covers for their books and place them in the school library so that other students can check them out. (If you are home schooling, pass the books around to other home-schooling families.)

Lives for Sale

See how many animals students can name that are slaughtered because human beings like to collect or buy products made from these animals (elephants—tusks, alligators—skin, rhinoceros—horn, morpho butterflies—wings). Have the students do research to uncover more species that are being threatened because of our need for trinkets. Students can write reports on the animals they choose, explaining the problems the animals are facing and what steps are being taken to save them.

What's Happening in Your Town?

Write to your state fish and wildlife department, college biology department, local conservation organization, nature sanctuary, or animal control officer. Ask the representative about threatened and/or vanishing species in your area. Invite the representative to visit and talk about his or her field and occupation.

The Bald Eagle

The bald eagle has long been a symbol of our country and its heritage. Just a few years ago, this bird was very nearly extinct. Now the bald eagle is slowly making a comeback. Ask the students to find out what caused their near-extinction and what has been done to increase their numbers.

Alligator Versus Crocodile

The alligator has often been hunted to use its skin for clothing accessories such as boots, purses, and belts. Ask students to find out why alligators are at risk but crocodiles are not. As a class, make a Venn Diagram comparing the characteristics of alligators and crocodiles:

- A Venn Diagram is made by drawing two circles that intersect (the right half of one circle overlaps the left half of the other). In the section of the circles that overlap, list characteristics of alligators and crocodiles that are the same.
- In the remainder of the left circle, list characteristics that belong only to the alligator. In the remainder of the right circle, list characteristics that belong only to the crocodile.

The American Bison

The American bison (or buffalo) is an important figure in the history of the United States. Have students write a report on the bison that tells why it was so important to Native Americans' way of life, what caused the demise of the buffalo, and what effect their extinction had on American history. Have students make a life cycle chart that describes the type of coat a bison wears in each season, its overall appearance, and the activities it engages in.

Sea Turtles

There are eight different species of sea turtles around the world. All but one of these species are endangered or threatened. Have students research a specific species of sea turtle. They should make a drawing of the species, show on a map where the species is located, learn about its life cycle, and give a class report on interesting facts about the turtle. They can also make a poster to remind others about the plight of the sea turtle. Then have students research the one species of sea turtle that is not endangered and try to determine why this species is not at risk. As a class, prepare a Venn Diagram comparing different species of turtles.

■ Creative Writing Activities

Following are instructions to give the students for various writing activities.

- What would it be like to be the last living human being on Earth? Write a week's worth of daily journal entries to record your lifestyle and your thoughts about your situation.

- Make a list of 10 endangered animals located throughout the world. You are in charge of their protection, but you have only limited funds to work with. Rank the animals in order of importance and give the reason for your rankings.

- You are the head of a worldwide commission responsible for improving the ecological status of the Earth. You must make important decisions on what steps should be taken to save the planet from eventual doom. You must also decide in what order these steps should be taken (i.e., what takes priority over what). Write a memorandum explaining which you believe is more important to save, endangered animals or plant life. Explain your decision in detail.

- Cut out several sheets of paper in the shape of any endangered animal. On each sheet of paper, write a fact about the endangered animal you choose. You may need to do some research to make sure you have facts for your book. When your facts are written down, you can illustrate each, bind the pages together, and then make a cover for your book in the shape of your animal.

- Imagine you are a young deer who has just experienced life in the woods on the first day of hunting season. Write a chronicle of your day and the feelings you experienced. (*The Gnats of Knotty Pine* by Peet)

- Pretend that you have just helped a group of neighbors who successfully freed a beached whale. You may need to do a little research on how such an effort is carried out. Write a story for your school newspaper detailing your experience. (*Humphrey the Lost Whale* by Tokuda; *Henry's Wrong Turn* by Ziefert and Baruffi.)

- Read *The Old Ladies Who Like Cats* by Greene. Develop your own story revolving around a small, mandated change in a community's lifestyle that had an unexpected effect on the ecological balance of the community.

- Do some research on the use of animals in laboratories to test medicines and other products for human use. After discussing the issues in class (older students could put on a debate), write down whether you think this practice is right or wrong. (*Chimpanzee Kid* by Roy)

- Write a slogan and put together a brochure aimed at convincing hunters to shoot animals with cameras instead of with guns. (*Lion on the Mountain* by Dixon)

- We frequently hear that the disappearance of a certain species of animal upsets the ecological balance of its habitat. Write a story about how the introduction of a new species into a habitat can cause similar problems. (*Donald and the Fish That Walked* by Riccuiti)

■ Art Activities

Following are instructions to give the students for various art activities.

- Draw a picture of an endangered animal. Cut out the animal and, with the other students, create a mural that has a large tree as the focal point. (*The Great Kapok Tree* by Cherry)

- Make a poster warning tourists to respect wild animals' rights and not to invade their habitat. You may want to include such rules as: "Don't feed the wild animals"; "Don't touch the animals"; and "Stay on marked trails while hiking." Try to think of other important rules hikers, tourists, and campers should observe when out in the wilderness. (*The Grizzly Sisters* by Bellows)

- Make a pop-up card of an endangered species to remind a friend or relative of its importance, using the following instructions:

    Fold a piece of paper in half lengthwise.

    About a quarter of the way down the fold, cut a 1.5-inch slit. Fold the paper back from the slit into small triangles.

    Unfold the paper, then fold it in half widthwise so that the slit faces you.

    Pull the top and bottom of the slit outward and fold the paper in half again to resemble a card, with the slit on the inside. Pull the triangles out, forming your animal's mouth.

    Draw and color (or add colored paper details to) an animal's face around the mouth you made.

    Add a message to your card.

- Make an ABC book of endangered, threatened, and/or extinct animals. For each letter of the alphabet, draw a picture of an animal that fits into one of the categories mentioned. Write the name of the animal below the picture and state which category the animal belongs in (endangered, threatened, or extinct).

- Make a puppet of an endangered animal out of recycled materials you find around the house (e.g., old socks, paper cups, felt, yarn, pipe cleaners, feathers, cotton balls, sequins). After your puppet is constructed, write a story about an adventure your endangered puppet had.

- Read *A Wolf Story* by McPhail. Make your own "Save the Wolf" posters and display them in your room.

- Cover old pin-on buttons with white contact paper or stick-on labels. Add your own drawing or message about the importance of protecting wildlife (or a specific animal).

- After discussing the dangers associated with throwing trash (especially plastic) in our oceans and lakes, draw a picture using the actual plastic item (six-pack rings, plastic bags, etc.) showing how it can be dangerous to a particular animal.

- Make endangered animal "bingo" cards. The letters across the top of the card should spell the name of an endangered animal. You can use different animals on each card. Each square on the bingo card (there is usually a row of five squares under each letter of the name, but you can make as many squares as you want to) should contain a fact about the animal such as how it looks, its feeding habits, or why it is endangered. Read a fact to the class and have them cover it, if it appears on their card. The first one to cover the required number of spaces yells out the name of the animal and is the winner.

- Make a diorama of an endangered animal showing the animal in the habitat that it would need to survive. To make a diorama:

    Cut one of the short ends out of a shoebox. Cut a square "window" in the middle of the other short end.

    On the inside of the box, facing the window, glue or tape pictures of the animal and its habitat into the scene that you want to make. You can draw the pictures yourself or cut pictures out of magazines. You may want to mount the pictures on cardboard before taping them inside your shoebox. You can also hang pictures from the inside of the top of the shoebox.

    When your scene is completed, tape some colored plastic wrap over the open end of the shoebox. Put your lid in place and look through the window at your scene.

Chapter 2
Diminishing Resources

■ Teaching Resources

Books containing experiment(s) relating to the subject matter are marked with a plus sign (+) before and after the title.

P   *Caring for Our Land,* by Carol Greene (Enslow, 1991)
Simplistic text and illustrations describe why land is important, what can happen to it, and what we can do to help.

P   *Dinosaurs to the Rescue! A Guide to Protecting Our Planet,* by Laurie Krasny Brown and Marc Brown (Little, Brown, 1994)
Dinosaur characters describe the Earth's major environmental problems: cars, electricity, plastic use, and lack of recycling, and suggest ways children can help.

P   *Famine and Hunger, Repairing the Damage,* by Lawrence Williams (New Discovery Books, 1992)
Informative text describes the causes of hunger and famine around the world and some of the ways of dealing with the problems.

P   *Recycle! A Handbook for Kids,* by Gail Gibbons (Little, Brown, 1996)
Describes the process of recycling from start to finish and discusses what happens to paper, glass, aluminum cans, and plastic when they are recycled into new products.

P   *Recycling,* by Joan Kalbacken and Emilie Lepthien (Children's Press, 1991)
Looks at how our garbage threatens the environment and wastes our resources. The advantages of recycling are also discussed, through simplistic text and color photographs.

P   *Window,* by Jeannie Baker (Puffin Books, 1991)
Good introduction to environmental concerns, through wordless collage pictures that follow a baby's view out a window as he grows older and the view changes.

P/I *At Home in the Rain Forest,* by Diane Willow (Charlesbridge, 1991)
Includes brief descriptions of plant and animal life in the Amazon rain forest, emphasizing the natural wonders of the rain forest. The book concludes with "Only people can save the rain forests."

P/I *Conservation,* by Richard Gates (Children's Press, 1982)
Explains how people have disrupted the ecological chain and offers ideas on what should be done to protect our natural resources.

P/I *Let's Talk Trash: The Kids' Book about Recycling,* by Kelly McQueen and David Fassler, M.D. (Waterfront Books, 1991)
Discusses the handling and recycling of trash using children's (ages 5–12) thoughts, questions, and drawings.

P/I *Life in the Oceans,* by Lucy Baker (Scholastic, 1993)
Concise text with nice illustrations looks at the plant life, animal life, and natural resources in the ocean. Also discusses the damage we are causing to the world's oceans.

P/I/U +*Earthwise at Home,*+ by Linda Lowery and Marybeth Lorbiecki (First Avenue Editions, 1992)
Discusses household ecology, including reusing, recycling, renewable energy, and smart shopping.

I *Captain Eco and the Fate of the Earth,* by Jonathan Porritt and Ellis Nadler (Dorling Kindersley, 1991)
Comic-like illustrations, with simple dialogue from Captain Eco and two friends, describe the Earth's environmental dangers and the need for change.

I *Caring for Planet Earth,* by Barbara Holland and Hazel Lucas (Chariot Victor, 1990)
Explores why we need to take care of our world, including recycling, how to protect endangered animals, why the balance of nature is important, and how we can save energy.

I *Compost Critters,* by Bianca Lavies (E. P. Dutton, 1993)
Explains what happens in a compost pile and how creatures, from bacteria and mites to millipedes and earthworms, aid in the process of turning compost into humus.

I *Conserving the Atmosphere,* by John Baines (Steck-Vaughn, 1993)
An introductory book on the problems of the Earth's atmosphere, fossil fuels, ozone layer destruction, radioactivity, and others. Also includes ideas on how to stop the destruction.

I +*Earthwise at Play,*+ by Linda Lowery and Marybeth Lorbiecki (Carolrhoda Books, 1992)
The interdependence of plants and animals, with activities that can help them and preserve them, are explored in this nicely done text.

I +*Earthwise at School,*+ by Linda Lowery and Marybeth Lorbiecki (Carolrhoda Books, 1993)
Earth facts are presented, with projects and activities to help protect the water, air, and land from pollution and destruction.

I *Farming and the Environment,* by Mark Lambert (Raintree, 1993)
Focuses on the impact of agriculture on the environment, along with current and future safe farming methods that could create a better future.

I *Garbage,* by Karen O'Connor (Lucent Books, 1989)
Describes dumping of garbage in oceans, on land, in the air, and in space, with suggestions to alleviate this problem of waste pollution. It is a part of the Our Endangered Planet series.

I   +*Looking at the Environment,*+ by David Suzuki (John Wiley & Sons, 1992)
Easy-to-read and understand text looks at the world around us, what ecology is, the water cycle, rain forest medicines, and other information on the interconnection of our earth, seas, and air.

I   *Oceans,* by Seymour Simon (Morrow Junior Books, 1990)
Explores the physical characteristics and life forms of the world's oceans and how easy it may be to destroy them.

I   *Our Endangered Planet: Groundwater,* by Mary Hoff and Mary M. Rodgers (Lerner, 1991)
Describes groundwater locations and properties, the uses and abuses of it worldwide, and ways to preserve this valuable resource through helpful, easy-to-read text and photographs. (Also available are *Our Endangered Planet: Atmosphere,* 1995; *Oceans,* 1991; *Life on Land,* 1992; *Rivers and Lakes,* 1991.)

I   *Population Growth,* by Suzanne Winckler and Mary M. Rodgers (Lerner, 1991)
Looks at the effects of uncontrolled population growth on natural resources, wildlife, and our environment. Has numerous helpful photographs.

I   *Squirmy Wormy Composters,* by Bobbie Kalman and Janine Schaub (Econo-Clad, 1999)
Describes worms as composters, as well as maintaining a compost pile.

I   *Tropical Rain Forests,* by Cornelia F. Mutel and Mary M. Rodgers (First Avenue Editions, 1993)
Contains numerous photographs and helpful text describing the rain forests, their environmental impact, and how humans have endangered the jungle ecosystem.

I   *Why Save the Rain Forest,* by Donald Silver (Messner, 1993)
Describes the rain forest habitats and locations, the dangers they face, and why we need to protect them, through nice illustrations and understandable text.

I   *World Water Watch,* by Michelle Koch (Greenwillow Books, 1993)
Brief text explains some dangers posed by humans to water animals.

I   *Worm's Eye View: Make Your Own Wildlife Refuge,* by Kipchak Johnson (Millbrook Press, 1991)
Explains the role of wild plants and animals in ecology and presents information on creating a wildlife refuge. The text is easy to read and has comic-like illustrations.

I/ U   *Discover Rain Forests,* by Lynne Hardie Baptista (Publications International, 1992)
Concise explanation of rain forests and their inhabitants. A good resource, with a glossary.

I/ U   +*50 Simple Things Kids Can Do to Recycle,*+ by Earth Works Group (Econo-Clad, 1994)
Information on recycling, protecting our resources, and protecting the planet.

I/ U   +*50 Simple Things Kids Can Do to Save the Earth,*+ by Earth Works Group (Econo-Clad, 1992)
Information on recycling, preserving our waterways, protecting animals, and protecting our resources.

I/ U   +*Keepers of the Earth,*+ by Michael J. Caduto and Joseph Bruchac (Fulcrum, 1991)
Native American stories from various tribes are accompanied by activities dealing with the environment. A teacher's guide is available.

I/ U   *Protecting the Oceans,* by John Baines (Raintree, 1990)
Describes the oceans' importance, the sources and effects of their pollution and misuse, and methods that are being used to protect them.

I/ U   +*Save Our Wetlands,*+ by Ron Hirschi (Delacorte Press, 1994)
Forest ecosystems are thoroughly covered by explaining the environmental concerns and historical background and by offering suggestions for creative activities.

U   *Caretakers of the Earth,* by Kathlyn Gay (Enslow, 1993)
Explains ways in which individuals and groups can help protect the environment, either locally or globally.

U   *Government and the Environment, Tracking the Record,* by Thomas G. Aylesworth (Enslow, 1993)
Looks at the history of environmental pollution, the growing awareness of the problem, and what steps the federal government is taking to protect the environment.

U   *The Greenhouse Effect, Life on a Warmer Planet,* by Rebecca L. Johnson (Lerner, 1994)
A thorough text on the research into and possible impact of the greenhouse effect.

U   +*Land Use and Abuse,*+ by Terri Willis (Children's Press, 1992)
Explains the ways in which people are harming the land and describes some methods of correcting and preventing these abuses. Well-done text with helpful illustrations and pictures.

U   *Rain Forests,* by Lois Warburton (Lucent, 1991)
Black-and-white photographs, with an in-depth text, depict native inhabitants, deforestation, and actions that can be taken for the preservation of the rain forests.

■ Reading Selections

Books marked with an asterisk (*) before and after the title are related to activities in the activity sections of this chapter.

A Family Goes Hunting, by Dorothy Hinshaw Patent (Clarion Books, 1991)
Shows the Cox family as they hunt for the food they eat. Presents safety and conservation principles that guide them. (Chapter Book)

Gift of the Tree, by Alvin Tresselt (Lothrop, Lee & Shepard, 1992)
Describes how animals depend on an old oak tree for shelter and food.

Great Trash Bash, by Loreen Leedy (Holiday House, 2000)
The animals of Beaston learn new ways to recycle and control their trash.

Journey of the Red-Eyed Tree Frog, by Martin Jordan and Tanis Jordan (Simon & Schuster, 1992)
A threatened tree frog journeys to the heart of the Amazon jungle to consult an Oracle Toad for advice on how to stop the destruction.

The Land of Gray Wolf, by Thomas Locker (Econo-Clad, 1999)
> Running Deer grows up watching white settlers claim his people's land, clear the forests, overfarm the land, and leave it when it is used up.

The Lost Lake, by Allen Say (Sandpiper Books, 1992)
> A young boy and his father plan a quiet trip to Lost Lake, only to find that the lake is noisy and overrun with visitors. As the two continue to seek their own special place, they grow closer and build a special bond.

Night Tree, by Eve Bunting (Voyager Picture Books, 1994)
> A family takes its annual trip into the woods to trim an evergreen for Christmas.

The Old Man and the Astronauts, by Ruth Tabrah (World Wide Distribution, 1975)
> An old man in New Guinea is worried that, as the astronauts remove rocks from the moon, it will provide less light.

Once There Was a Tree, by Gennadi Spirin (E. P. Dutton, 1992)
> An old stump attracts people and other living creatures and, when it is gone, a new tree takes its place.

Once There Was a Tree, by Natalia Romanova (E. P. Dutton, 1992)
> The story of the stump of a tree that is split by lightning and then felled by a woodcutter. Many animals make use of the stump and try to claim it but find that it is part of the Earth, which belongs to all of us.

Places of Refuge, by Dorothy Hinshaw Patent (Houghton Mifflin, 1992)
> Tells how wildlife refuges use methods to maintain a natural balance with the environment. (Chapter Book)

Pumpkins: A Story for a Field, by Mary Lyn Ray (Harcourt Brace Jovanovich, 1992)
> When a man harvests and sells a large crop of pumpkins, he is able to save his field from developers.

A River Dream, by Allen Say (Houghton Mifflin, 1993)
> A young boy must decide whether to keep his prize fishing catch or return it to the river that it came from.

A Rose for Abby, by Donna Guthrie (Abingdon Press, 1998)
> After seeing a homeless woman searching for food on her street, Abby decides to prepare a dinner for the homeless people of her neighborhood.

Someday a Tree, by Eve Bunting (Clarion Books, 1996)
> Suddenly, in the middle of spring, the leaves on Alice's favorite tree turn brown and fall off. The reasons teach Alice a valuable lesson.

Song of the Trees, by Mildred D. Taylor (Laureleaf, 1996)
> A rural family tries to save the forest on their land when an unscrupulous man tries to cut it down.

Stay Away from the Junkyard, by Tricia Tusa (Econo-Clad, 1999)
> Theo finds out how to turn junk into beauty when he helps out a junkman and his pig.

A Tree Is Nice, by Janice May Udry (HarperCollins Juvenile Books), 1988
> A young child gives several reasons why a tree is nice to have around.

Where the Forest Meets the Sea, by Jeannie Baker (Greenwillow, 1988)
> A father takes his son on a camping trip into the Australian rain forest. While there, the son thinks about the past of the plants and animals and wonders if they will have a future.

The following books are out of print, but may be available at the local library.

Eli's Song, by Monte Killingsworth (Margaret K. McElderry, 1985)
> Twelve-year-old Eli tries to save the trees of a nearby forest from being destroyed. (Chapter Book)

Greening the City Streets, by Barbara Huff (Houghton Mifflin, 1990)
> Shows how people of all ages and abilities become involved in the community's garden movement.

The Little Park, by Dale Fife (Whitman, 1973)
> Neighborhood children work to preserve their last vacant lot as a wildlife preserve.

Mousekin's Lost Woodland, by Edna Miller (Simon & Schuster, 1992)
> When a new house is built in the woods, many trees are removed, and the animals' homes are destroyed. Luckily, Mousekin finds one home that respects Nature.

Rads, Ergs, and Cheeseburgers, by Bill Yanda (Muir, 1991)
> A visit to a planet where the inhabitants did not learn in time to use their energy resources wisely.

Squirrel Park, by Lisa Ernst (Bradbury Press, 1993)
> Beavers build a dam that creates a pond that is beneficial to many different creatures.

Stop that Noise!, by Paul Geraghty (Crown Publishers, 1992)
> A mouse is no longer annoyed by the sounds of the forest once he has heard the sounds of a machine that has come to knock down the trees.

The Town That Moved, by Mary Jane Finsand (Carolrhoda Books, 1983)
> When iron ore is discovered under a Minnesota town, the people decide to move the town rather than have it destroyed.

The Tree, by Naomi Russell (E. P. Dutton, 1989)
> A squirrel leaves behind an acorn from his pile, and a huge tree grows. After the tree is cut down, another acorn is left behind.

What I Did Last Summer, by Glory St. John (Atheneum, 1978)
> A family decides not to use any utilities all summer long and to rise and retire with the sun. (Chapter Book)

■ Science Activities

Packaging Demonstration

- Ask each child in the class to bring in an unopened, packaged grocery item (box of cookies, box of crackers, package of rice, etc.). Open each package and remove the contents. Talk about how the contents are packaged. How many different types of wrapping are involved? How large is the outside box as compared to the contents?

- Get two grocery bags and unwrap the food items. Place the packaging in one grocery bag and the food in the other. Compare how much packaging (and waste) is involved in the products we purchase at the grocery store.

- Have the children design new packaging that will protect the food sufficiently but create less waste. If you have what you feel is a viable alternative to a product's current packaging, let the children write to the manufacturer suggesting the revised packaging.

Paper Production

Have students research how paper is made and why there are different types and qualities of paper, then try to make their own paper using the following instructions:

- Blend small scraps of newspaper (one sheet) with two cups of warm water in a blender or food processor. Add two teaspoons of liquid starch.
- Spread this pulp over a screen that has been placed in the bottom of a cake pan. Lift out the screen and let the mixture drain into the cake pan for about one minute.
- Place several newspapers in a pile and put a paper towel on top of them. Set the screen (pulp side up) on the paper and top with another paper towel. Place more newspapers on top of that. Roll with a rolling pin to remove excess water.
- Carefully remove the top newspapers. Turn the pile over and remove all of the newspapers, paper towels, and the screen.
- Put a dry paper towel on top of the pulp that is remaining and let it sit for 24 hours to dry.
- Remove the paper towel.

Ecological Bingo

- Reinforce ecology terms by playing "ecological bingo."
- On separate slips of paper (or on index cards), write down an ecology term with its definition.
- On a blackboard or easel, list the terms you are using, such as *air, waste, pollution, biodegradable, compost, endangered, conserve, energy, decompose, litter, landfill, methane, recycle, trash, water, aluminum, ecology, deplete, disposable, dump, toxic, hazardous, natural resource, non-renewable resource, organic,* and *Styrofoam.*
- On pieces of cardboard, draw a grid with 25 squares (or use old cards from a bingo game). Write one of the terms listed on the board in each square of the card until it is filled.
- To play, the "caller" uses the slips of paper to read the definition of a term to the players. The players must determine which term the definition refers to and cover it if it appears on their cards. When a player gets five squares in a row covered, the player calls "bingo." Check the terms on the player's card with the definitions you have called to see if he or she is a winner.

Careers

- Ask the students to research what kinds of careers are available in the area of conservation. They should look into different areas of our society that are involved in helping to protect our environment and recycling products and answer these questions: What types of careers are associated with this work? What educational background is required to work in these industries? Tell them not to forget to look into the government agencies that are responsible for protecting the environment.
- Have students investigate the products that are derived from recycled materials and answer these questions: Which types of companies are involved in producing these by-products? Which areas of study would best prepare you for a career in conservation?

Bags, Bags, and More Bags

- Have students track how many paper and plastic bags their families use and dispose of in a two-week period. They should count every grocery bag, department store bag, lunch bag, and paper and plastic bag, then write down a list of ways in which their families could put these bags to use so that they would not just be thrown away. Ask students to come up with ways to recycle the plastic or paper bags they get from the stores or devise other methods of carrying items.

- In many countries and cities, residents bring their own bags to the supermarket when shopping. Ask students to check to see if their local supermarket sells cloth shopping bags or if it gives shoppers money off the grocery bill for each paper or plastic bag they bring in to use to carry groceries home. Ask the students: If you used cloth shopping bags or reused your old paper or plastic bags, how many new bags would you save in a year's time?

Plant a Tree

As a class, plant a "living memorial." Plant a tree sapling in the schoolyard or have students plant one in their own yards. Dedicate the tree to someone who has influenced your students' lives, or to a cause such as "a better tomorrow." Have the students care for the tree and take pictures of it as it grows through each season. Although your students will move on to other classes, you can put a bulletin board outside your classroom so that they can keep track of the progress of "their" tree.

Old for New

- Ask students to bring in items that their families are throwing away. As a money-making project, have the students come up with ways to transform this "trash" into useful items that they can sell. They could make pencil holders, note pads, picture frames, bird feeders, and so forth.

- As a community project, see if the students can come up with things to make from this "trash" that would be of use to a nearby retirement or nursing home, a homeless shelter, or some other organization in your community.

Recycling

- Recyclable materials are usually divided into four major groups: paper, glass, plastic, and metal. Have students choose one of the groups and research the recycling process. You could do this as a group project, dividing the class into four groups. Ask students to find out what natural resources are used to make the product, what the recycling process for this material is, and what new products can be made when the original product is recycled.

- Write to a manufacturer of the product you chose requesting production and recycling information. (For example, you might write to the Steel Can Recycling Institute, 680 Anderson Dr., Pittsburgh, PA 15220 for information on how to recycle steel.) Ask the students to follow through on the suggestions you receive from the manufacturer.

Aluminum

Many items can be recycled today, and aluminum is one product that we can all recycle. However, some cans are not aluminum. Gather several metal items, such as tin cans, aluminum cans, nails, bottle caps, and paper clips. Using a magnet, demonstrate to the class which items are magnetic and which are not. Ask students how this knowledge can help consumers decide what can and cannot be recycled. (Some soda cans will claim to be recyclable but may be rejected by recycling centers. These cans contain other metals besides aluminum to give them extra strength. These cans are magnetic.)

U. S. National Forests

Have the students do a historical study of various laws passed by Congress to manage and conserve U. S. national forests. Some of the applicable laws are listed below.

1911—The Weeks Law

1924—The Clarke-McNary Act

1964—The Wilderness Act

1974—The Forest and Rangeland Renewable Resources Planning Act

Do Your Part

As a group, brainstorm ways in which you can conserve our diminishing resources. Select four or five of the ideas that you think are realistic to do immediately. Make a chart that lists the ideas your class has selected across the top and the days of the week for a one-week period down the side. Keep track of how you all do each day in your efforts to conserve these resources.

Hot Dogs Anyone?

After discussing the uses of solar energy, make a "solar-powered hot dog cooker" and make lunch for the class.

- Cover the outside of a shoebox with black paper. Line the inside of the box with aluminum foil, shiny side up.
- Poke a hole in each of the short ends of the shoebox and insert a piece of hanger, a skewer, or a thin dowel rod between the two holes.
- Put one or two hot dogs on the rod lengthwise.
- Drape a piece of foil shiny side up over the top of the shoebox.
- Cover the box with plastic wrap and place the whole thing in full sunlight for approximately three hours. When the hotdogs are cooked completely, they can be eaten.

Water Conservation

Divide students into teams and find a sink. While one child brushes his or her teeth, have another child catch the running water in a container. Measure the amount of water used. Repeat the process, but have the children turn off the water when it is not actually being used. Compare the amount of water used this time with the amount used in the exercise above. Discuss other ways to conserve water. Have each student write down as many ideas as possible and then discuss them in class.

Conservation Calculations

- We would save 500,000 trees every week if everyone recycled the Sunday newspaper. Have the class determine how many trees would be saved if every member of the class recycled the newspaper for a month, every house in the neighborhood recycled newspapers for six months, and one child in the class recycled the newspaper for one year.
- Every minute, 100 acres of rain forest are destroyed. Have students calculate how many acres are destroyed during recess time, while they are eating their lunch, during the time they spend doing schoolwork, and so forth. For older students, you can find the number of acres in your state, county, or city and determine how much of the area is destroyed every minute.

Hunger

Contact UNICEF and ask for information on their Halloween campaign. If possible, you could decide to participate in their endeavor. They will send you a great deal of information about world hunger. Discuss this information and what is causing so much hunger in the world. Have the students write down all the food they eat in one day's time and describe what items were necessary for basic survival and what could have been eliminated. (*A Rose for Abby* by Guthrie)

Should It Be Law?

The Water Quality Act of September 1965 is written up in the *World Almanac* and the *Environmental Quality Index*. Get a copy of the Act, then read it to the class and discuss it. Ask students to imagine that this Act is up for renewal and write an essay giving reasons why they would support its renewal or why they think the Act should be repealed.

We Can Make It Happen!

Investigate whether your town has any designated areas where flowers are planted every year. Sometimes garden clubs and church groups "sponsor" a garden and plant the flowers. Find out if your class or support group could sponsor a flower garden somewhere in your community. (*Greening the City Streets* by Huff)

■ Creative Writing Activities

Following are instructions to give the students for various writing activities.

- You have won a trip for you and a companion to go on a tour of a tropical rain forest in South America. You won the trip by writing a 15-minute children's show, in storyboard form, to convince your peers of the importance of the rain forests to their future and of their responsibility in preserving them. Create the award-winning storyboard. (A storyboard shows dialogue for a television show written beneath a square that contains a picture of what will be on screen while the dialogue is being heard. On an 8 1/2-by-11-inch piece of paper, you can probably fit nine picture squares—three rows of three—with room for the dialogue beneath each one.) Write an account of your trip for your other classmates or friends detailing the things you saw and learned. (*Journey of the Red-Eyed Tree Frog* by Jordan and Jordan)

- Write a letter to your representative expressing your concern over the deforestation of our natural forests. Topics you could discuss include excessive clear-cutting; pollution of the rivers, lakes, and creeks that currently exist in the forests; and destruction of fishing grounds and game preserves.

- Suppose that we had put such a strain on our supply of electricity that it was being rationed. You could use only so much electricity each month and had to learn to use it wisely so that your allotment was not used up before the month was over. Make a list of all of the ways in which you and your family use electricity in your home. Rank these uses by level of importance. Write up a report recommending which uses of electricity should be abandoned; which need to be curtailed, and by how much; and which are fine as they are. Be specific about exactly how long each appliance can be used in a month's time. (*The Old Man and the Astronauts* by Tabrah)

- Write a detective story to solve the mystery of why the leaves on your favorite tree have suddenly turned brown and fallen off. Assume it is not fall! (*Someday a Tree* by Bunting)

- What would it be like if we had a permanent power shortage and had to live without electricity? Would our lifestyle resemble that of the pioneers? How would it be similar, and how would it be different? (*What I Did Last Summer* by St. John)

- Put together a comprehensive advertising campaign aimed at informing the public about our dwindling natural resources and letting them know what they can do to help. You will need to decide what particular audience you want to target (adults over 25, teens, elementary school children, senior citizens, etc.). Then decide what media you will use to get your message across (television, magazines, newspapers, direct mailings, etc.). What will be the focus of your campaign (water, forests, mineral resources, a combination of several topics)? After you have made your decisions, write the actual content of your ad(s). Will you have some kind of symbol or spokesperson to associate with your campaign? (Younger students can simply write a story telling about the need to save our natural resources and make a picture or poster to accompany it.) (*The Little Park* by Fife)

■ Art Activities

Following are instructions to give the students for various art activities.

- The forest is one of our most valuable resources. "Recycle" old magazines into forest scene works of art.

  Paint the background scene of a forest on a piece of white paper or poster board.

  Page through old magazines to find objects that are the same color as the animals, trees, bushes, and so forth, that you want to put in your forest scene. The magazine objects can be anything, as long as they are the color that you are looking for.

  Cut the magazine picture into tiny pieces. Arrange these pieces to form the objects you want in your picture. (A picture of a brown suitcase could be rearranged into the trunk of a tree; a picture of a green sweater could be made into the leaves.)

  The resulting picture will look somewhat mosaic. (*The Land of Gray Wolf* by Locker; *A Tree Is Nice* by Udry)

- Find different pieces of paper that have different textures (typing paper, construction paper, sandpaper, tracing paper, etc.) Make a picture by cutting figures or shapes out of the different-textured papers and pasting them in a design on a piece of poster board.

- Make a notepad to recycle paper, using the following instructions:

  On a piece of cardboard (poster board or the scraps of an old cereal box, etc.) draw the outline of a leaf, acorn, or pine cone. Cut out the object and use paints and markers to color it in. Your finished product should be approximately 6 inches square so that the notepaper fits on top of it.

  Cut 12 to 15 3-1/2-inch squares out of paper that has been used on just one side (old computer paper, completed ditto sheets, etc.).

  Put the squares in a pile and staple them to your cardboard cutout in the top right-hand and left-hand corners. You now have a notepad that can be replenished in the same way whenever you run out of paper. (*The Tree* by Russell)

- Draw a line lengthwise down a sheet of 8 1/2-by-11-inch paper. On the left-hand side of the paper, draw a scene showing a child or adult misusing one of our natural resources (bulldozing trees, leaving the tap water running, leaving lights burning unnecessarily, etc.). On the right-hand side of the paper, draw the same scene but with the child or adult handling the situation properly. Try to come up with a title for each column of your paper (e.g., "Negative and Positive," "Dufus and Cool"). (*Journey of the Red-Eyed Frog* by Jordan and Jordan)

- Make a scrapbook or autograph book using an old cereal box and grocery bags, as follows:

  For the cover and binding, cut away the top and sides of the cereal box. Trim the remainder of the box (the front and back connected by the bottom panel) to the size you want (suggested size: front cover would be 7 inches long and 6 inches wide).

Cover your book with old wallpaper or gift wrap (the more colorful, the better).

Cut pieces from grocery bags so they will fit inside your book (about 6 1/2 by 5 1/2 inches).

Punch two holes in the front and back covers (close to the binding) and in the left-hand side of the pages so that the holes in the covers and the holes in the pages match up.

Put your book together. Feed a shoelace through the holes to hold the book together and tie it in a bow at the front of the book.

- Use a paper plate and materials you find around your house or school to make animal masks. Try to be as creative as possible in using unusual items that are recyclable. Write a short skit, with an ecological theme, about the animal you have re-created.

- As a class, create a bulletin board around the "three R's": Reduce, Reuse, and Recycle. You will be assigned the task of obtaining information from a particular organization and preparing suggestions based on the literature you gather on how students can make a difference ecologically. Every two or three weeks a small group of students will be made responsible for re-doing the bulletin board. When it's your turn, you should have new information to put up plus artwork and suggestions that match your theme.

- Read the poem, "Sarah Cynthia Sylvia Stout Would Not Take the Garbage Out" found in the collection of poems, *Where The Sidewalk Ends* by Silverstein. Draw a picture of garbage on a piece of construction paper or on poster board. Draw, find, or make garbage to illustrate the poem you read. Come up with creative ideas for making your own wrapping paper for presents. Some examples follow:

Use colorful comics as they are, or cut out pictures of the colored comics and glue them onto sheets of black-and-white comics for a unique look.

Decorate a paper bag (lunch bag or grocery bag) with odds and ends such as sequins, pom-poms, yarn, fabric, feathers, or buttons.

Cut a sponge or a potato into a shape (star, diamond, circle, etc.), dip it in tempera paint, and "stamp" on a plain piece of paper. Other "stamps" include a potato masher, a shell, a jar lid, a cookie cutter, forks, and feathers.

- Recycle cardboard tubes from paper towel, wrapping paper, and toilet paper rolls by making napkin holders using the following instructions:

Cut the tubes into 2-inch lengths.

Tear different-colored tissue paper into strips or squares. Dip the strips or squares in thinned-down, white glue or liquid starch.

Squeeze off the excess liquid and cover the cardboard tubes with the paper.

Add sequins, beads, rhinestones, or yarn after the tissue paper dries to make the holder even fancier. (*Great Trash Bash* by Leedy)

- Make an indoor compost holder by cutting the top off of a one-gallon plastic milk jug. (Requires adult supervision of younger students.) Start your cut at the top of the bottle, between the spout and the handle of the jug. Cut down on both sides of the bottle in an "S" shape that meets at the front of the bottle. The two cuts should meet about one-third of the way down the front of the bottle. Remove the part of the bottle you have cut away. Using permanent marker, decorate the jug however you want to. Keep the jug near the sink in your kitchen and fill it with food scraps that can then be carried out to a compost heap in your backyard.

Chapter 3
Pollution

■ Teaching Resources

Books containing experiment(s) relating to the subject matter are marked with a plus sign (+) before and after the title.

P   +*Acid Rain,*+ by John Baines (Steck-Vaughn, 1990)
Describes, through brief text and numerous illustrations, the causes of acid rain, solutions to the problem, and actions being taken.

P   *Dinosaurs to the Rescue! A Guide to Protecting Our Planet,* by Laurie Krasny Brown & Marc Brown (Little, Brown, 1994)
Dinosaur characters describe the Earth's major environmental problems: cars, electricity, plastic use, and lack of recycling, and suggests ways children can help.

P   *For the Love of Our Earth,* by P. K. Hallinan (Ideals Children's Books, 2000)
Illustrations and rhyming verse show children working together for the betterment of our world by fighting pollution.

P   +*Starting Science: Waste,*+ by Kay Davies and Wendy Oldfield (Raintree Steck-Vaughn, 1991)
Discusses numerous aspects of waste and pollution, with simplistic text.

P   *Where Does the Garbage Go?,* by Paul Showers (HarperCollins, 1994)
Explains that people create too much waste and how waste is now recycled and put into landfills.

P/I *Air Pollution, a New True Book,* by Darlene R. Stille (Children's Press, 1990)
Easy-to-read text about the air's benefits, its pollution, and the harmful consequences of pollution, with suggestions for avoiding it.

P/I *Caring for Our Air,* by Carol Greene (Enslow, 1991)
Simple text tells about the ecological issue of air pollution and presents ideas on how to help control the problem.

P/I *The Greenhouse Effect,* by Darlene R. Stille (Children's Press, 1990)
Easy-to-read text explains the causes and effects of the greenhouse effect, plus suggestions for stopping it.

P/I *The River,* by David Bellamy (Antique Collectors Club Books, 1999)
Story about pond life and the effects of human-made catastrophes on it told through easy text and watercolor illustrations.

P/I *Trash!,* by Charlotte Wilcox (Carolrhoda Books, 1988)
Brief text, with excellent photographs, describes the various methods of garbage disposal, emphasizing sanitary landfills; includes information on alternatives.

P/I/U +*Earthwise at School,*+ by Linda Lowery and Marybeth Lorbiecki (Carolrhoda Books, 1993)
Presents facts about planet Earth and suggests projects and activities to help protect the water, air, and land from pollution. Discusses developing an action plan for local environmental improvement.

I *The Environment and Health,* by Brian R. Ward (Franklin Watts, 1989)
Examines the numerous things in our environment that threaten our health, such as noise, water and air pollution, radiation, cigarettes, lead and asbestos, sun, stress, and accidents.

I *Oil Spills,* by Laurence Pringle (Morrow Junior Books, 1993)
Provides information on petroleum and its uses, the effects of oil spills, and how these disasters can be prevented and cleaned up.

I *Our Endangered Planet: Rivers and Lakes,* by Mary Hoff and Mary M. Rodgers (Lerner, 1991)
Informs the reader about the dangers of surface water pollution and the global importance of keeping the water clean.

I *Our Global Greenhouse,* by April Koral (Franklin Watts, 1991)
Describes the origins, possible consequences, and prevention of the greenhouse effect.

I *The River,* by David Bellamy (Antique Collectors Club Books, 1999)
Describes how plants and animals exist in a river environment following a human-made catastrophe.

I +*Wonderful Water,*+ by Bobbie Kalman and Janine Schaub (Crabtree, 1992)
Concentrates on all forms of water, the water cycle and sources, water pollution, and conservation.

I/U *Complete Trash: the Best Way to Get Rid of Practically Everything Around the House,* by Norman Crampton (M. Evans, 1989)
Presents an alphabetical listing of how to dispose of household items, including alternatives for burning, burying, recycling, or composting.

I/U *Environmental Awareness: Solid Waste,* by Mary Ellen Snodgrass (Bancroft-Sage, 1991)
Describes the management of many types of solid waste and the hazards they pose, along with guidelines for waste reduction.

I/U *Facts on Domestic Waste and Industrial Pollutants,* by Hugh Johnstone (Franklin Watts, 1990)
Examines the growing problem of waste disposal and alternatives to such methods as landfills and garbage dumps.

I/U *Our Endangered Planet: Rivers and Lakes,* by Mary Hoff and Mary M. Rodgers (Lerner, 1991)
Alerts the reader to the dangers of surface water pollution and the global imperative to keep these waters clean.

I/U *Our Poisoned Sky,* by Edward F. Dolan (Cobblehill Books, 1991)
Describes the effects of pollutants on our environment and what is being done to prevent further destruction.

I/U *Protecting the Oceans,* by John Baines (Steck-Vaughn, 1991)
Numerous illustrations and concise text describe the importance of oceans, the pollution and misuse of them, and ways to protect them.

I/U +*What a Load of Trash!,*+ by Steve Skidmore (Millbrook Press, 1991)
Informative, fun-to-read text, with appealing illustrations, describes the different kinds of wastes and their environmental effects.

U *The Bhopal Chemical Leak,* by Arthur Diamond (Lucent, 1990)
A thorough description of events leading up to and following the world's largest chemical disaster brings to light many issues involving chemicals and the safety of the Earth and its people.

U *Garbage: Understanding Words in Context,* by Robert Anderson (Greenhaven Press, 1991)
Four questions about recycling and trash are answered from two different viewpoints.

■ Reading Selections

Books marked with an asterisk (*) before and after the title are related to activities in the activity sections of this chapter.

Brother Eagle, Sister Sky, by Susan Jeffers (Dial Books for Young Readers, 1991)
>   The Native American belief that the Earth and all of its creatures are sacred is the central theme of this story, which cautions all people to preserve our environment.

Farewell to Shady Glade, by Bill Peet (Econo-Clad, 1999)
>   Old Raccoon decides that he and his friends must leave Shady Glade when men with bulldozers arrive and start leveling the trees nearby.

Great Trash Bash, by Loreen Leedy (Holiday House, 1991)
>   The animals of Beaston learn new ways to recycle and control their trash.

Just a Dream, by Chris Van Allsburg (Houghton Mifflin, 1990)
>   After Walter has a nightmare about how the world will be in the future, he agrees to stop littering and to help with the family's recycling efforts.

The Lorax, by Theodor Geisel (Dr. Seuss) (Random House, 1998)
>   The local pollution problem is detailed by the Once-ler.

Michael Bird-Boy, by Tomie de Paola (Aladdin, 1987)
>   A large, black cloud makes many harmful environmental changes in a child's environment. He helps to solve the problem when he locates the source of the pollution.

Miss Rumphius, by Barbara Cooney (Econo-Clad, 1999)
>   Miss Rumphius grows up remembering her grandfather's directive that she must "do something to make the world more beautiful while you are here on Earth."

The Paper Bag Prince, by Colin Thompson (Dragonfly, 1997)
>   An old man moves into an abandoned train at the dump and watches nature reclaim the polluted land.

A Pocketful of Cricket, by Rebecca Caudill (Econo-Clad, 1999)
>A little boy who loves nature and the world around him learns to share this love with others.

Professor Noah's Spaceship, by Brian Wildsmith (Oxford University Press, 1985)
>Various animals help Professor Noah build a spaceship to escape the pollution destroying their habitats. Instead of reaching another planet, however, they travel backward through time to a pre-industrial Earth.

Seeds of Change, by Sarah Sargent (Bradbury Press, 1989)
>Rachel is torn between the beauty of the swamp and her father's desire to drain it and make it into a theme park. (Chapter Book)

Sign of the Seashore, by Graeme Base (Abradale Press, 1998)
>The sea life of a coral reef is threatened when a real-estate deal fills their world with poisonous waste.

Someday a Tree, by Eve Bunting (Clarion Books, 1993)
>Neighbors unite to try to save an old oak tree poisoned by pollution.

And Still the Turtle Watched, by Sheila MacGill-Callahan (Econo-Clad, 1999)
>A turtle, carved in a rock by Indians centuries earlier, watches sadly as humans come, bringing many changes with them.

Stop That Noise!, by Paul Geraghty (Millbrook Press, 1998)
>A tree mouse starts to appreciate the forest noises around her after hearing the noise made by a machine that is destroying the forest.

Talking Earth, by Jean Craighead George (Harper Trophy, 1987)
>Billie Wind ventures into the Everglades and learns the importance of listening to the Earth's messages. (Chapter Book)

The Wartville Wizard, by Don Madden (Econo-Clad, 1999)
>An old man tries to fight a town full of litterbugs by sending each piece of litter back to the person who tossed it.

Who Really Killed Cock Robin, by Jean Craighead George (HarperCollins, 1991)
>Tony, an eighth-grader, follows many environmental clues to try to find out what killed a town robin. (Chapter Book)

The Wump World, by Bill Peet (Houghton Mifflin, 1981)
>The Wump World is turned into a concrete jungle after it is invaded by the Pollutians.

Zebo and the Dirty Planet, by Kim Fernandes (Annick Press, 1991)
>A story with a Noah's Ark theme that tells of a space traveler bringing animals from a polluted planet to his own clean planet to help them survive.

The following books are out of print, but may be available at the local library.

The Hidden Jungle, by Simon Henwod (Farrar, Straus & Giroux, 1992)
>Mr. Pinn must find a new home for a potted tree that is dying from the city's noise, dirt, and odor.

Jack, the Seal, and the Sea, by Gerald Aschenbrenner (Silver Burdett, 1988)
>Jack, a fisherman, is oblivious to the pollution in the sea until he comes across a young seal who is dying because of it.

Lake Fear, by Ian McMahan (Macmillan, 1985)

    Ricky and Alec uncover a case of chemical pollution and computer fraud while searching for the source of a strange disease. (Chapter Book)

Shadows on the Pond, by Alison Herzig (Little, Brown, 1985)

    Intruders threaten to destroy the beaver pond which is Jill's refuge when she is troubled. (Chapter Book)

Song of the Smoggy Stars, by Osmond Molarsky (H. Z. Walck, 1972)

    A fourth-grader is inspired to write a song against air pollution after experiencing the clear air of the mountains. (Chapter Book)

A Tale of Antarctica, by Ulco Glimmerveen (Scholastic, 1989)

    Penguins in Antarctica demonstrate how their environment is threatened by the pollution from humans' presence.

Ultramarine, by Jenny Nimmo (Dutton Childrens Books, 1992)

    A brother and sister learn about their true past from a stranger who helps them rescue birds from an oil spill. (Chapter Book)

■ Science Activities

Water Filtration

- As a class, create your own water-filtering system using the following instructions:

    Place a coffee filter inside a funnel and place the funnel in a jar.

    Place some pebbles inside the filter and some sand on top of the pebbles.

    Pour some muddy water into the funnel and watch the water come out the other end. (Repeat, if necessary.)

    What changes do you see in the water? How is this process used today?

- Use the following experiment to find out how water treatment plants remove dirt and particles from the water:

    Take a two-liter soda bottle and cut off the top of the bottle (about 5 inches from the top).

    Remove the bottle's cap, invert the 5-inch section you cut off, and place it over the bottom section of the bottle.

    Place a coffee filter inside the inverted section of the bottle. Layer the coffee filter with 1/2 cup of sand; two or three briquettes of charcoal, crushed; and another layer (about 1 1/2 inches deep) of sand.

    Pour some dirty water over the three layers in the coffee filter and observe the water as it comes out of the filter.

    Does the water look different than it did when you poured it in the top of the filter? Would this water be fit to drink? (No! It may still contain harmful germs. Chlorine is added to our drinking water to kill germs.)

Biodegradable?

Have students place several items (such as salt, sugar, oil, paper, wood, leaves, Styrofoam, or crackers) into separate jars and cover the items with water. They should label the contents of each jar. Ask them to record their observations of the jars for a day or two. Then have them vigorously shake the jars and record their observations again. Ask them what it means when a substance is *biodegradable* or *non-biodegradable* and what products we should be careful about buying or discarding.

Decomposition

Ask the students to predict the rate of decomposition of several different types of trash (e.g., Styrofoam, a plastic spoon, chicken bones, newspaper, a sliver of wood, a piece of bread). Take several 2-liter soda bottles and cut off the top section of each. Ask the students to fill each bottle partially with soil, then place a sample of each of the types of trash in a separate bottle on top of the soil and cover the items with more dirt. They should label the contents of each bottle. Have the students add water to the dirt and set the bottles in a place where they will be exposed to sunlight. After two weeks, have them unearth the samples they buried and record any changes. The students should then replant the samples and continue to unearth them for the next several months, noting what has decomposed and at what rate. After they have checked the samples several times, ask students for suggestions about what might quicken the decomposition process. Try those suggestions that you think have merit.

Consider having an expert speak to the class on composting and how to make a compost bin for use at home. Would different types of soil or different areas (grasslands versus desert) decompose items at different rates?

Toxins

- Discuss what alternatives we can use to decrease the amount of toxins in the air. For example, the gas in aerosol cans can harm our ozone layer. Ask the students what products come in spray form and what alternatives we could use.

- What cleaning products do we have that may harm our environment? Ask the students to try this alternative to commercial window cleaners: Mix a solution of half water and half vinegar. Spray it on the glass surface and wipe with a newspaper. The newspaper will even leave an invisible film to resist dust.

- Wash a window in your classroom. Use a popular window cleaner on one half and the water-and-vinegar mixture described above on the other half. Ask the students to assess how well each product cleans. After a couple of days, is one half of the window any cleaner than the other?

Oil Spill

Demonstrate an oil spill to the students using the following instructions:

- Add a small amount of motor or vegetable oil to a shallow pan of water. Stir the water to distribute the oil throughout. Drop several items, such as rocks, sticks, and feathers, into the water. After the items are covered with the mixture, try to clean them off. How easy or difficult is it to get the items clean? Discuss how actual oil spills can affect the environment and the animals they come in contact with.

- In another shallow pan of water, add a small amount of motor or vegetable oil. Have the students try to come up with ways to clean up the oil spill, such as scooping it up, blowing it away, or absorbing it with paper towels. Try some of the methods and determine which are most effective. Have the students investigate what methods are being used by industries today and how effective they are.

More with Oil

As a demonstration, fill a glass container halfway with vegetable oil. Stir in a generous amount of dark food coloring to simulate an "oil spill." Place a hard-boiled egg in the oil spill to show the harmful effects of oil. Cover the egg well with the liquid and allow it to float for at least 30 minutes. While you are waiting, have the students predict what, if anything, will happen to the egg as a result of floating in the oil spill. Record their predictions. Remove the egg after the 30 minutes and dry it. Have the students observe what the outside of the egg looked like immediately after being removed and, in more detail, after the egg has been dried. Record their observations. Peel the shell off the egg and note any further observations. Compare the actual results of the experiment with the students' predictions. (Eggshells are naturally porous, so oils and other dangerous poisons, like insecticides, can be life-threatening to animals and plants.)

Chlorofluorocarbons

Discuss chlorofluorocarbons (CFCs), which are chemicals made by people. They are unchanged close to the Earth, but higher in the atmosphere they have created a hole in the ozone layer. Have students look around their homes for products and appliances that still contain CFCs. Make a chart of the students' findings and discuss what they could substitute for these products.

Test Your Air

Cut out several cardboard strips, each approximately 3 by 12 inches. In each strip, cut out three or four holes the size of a quarter. Cover one side of each hole with tape so that the holes have the sticky side of the tape exposed. Have the students hang these strips outside in several different locations. Leave the strips hanging for seven to ten days. Have the students collect the strips and look at the tape. They may need to hold them up to a light or lay them on white paper to see better. Have them use a magnifying glass to observe more closely. How clean is the air outside? Was there one area that was dirtier than others?

Pollution Password

On separate slips of paper, write a term that has to do with pollution (greenhouse effect, rain forests, carbon dioxide, littering, oil spills, global warming, etc.). Include the definition for the word on the slip of paper. Divide the class into teams and play "Pollution Password." One person on each team looks at the word on the slip. Taking turns, team members give a one-word clue to another person on the team in an attempt to get him or her to say the word in question. Whichever team says the word first is the winner. You can give out one point per word and play for as long as you like.

The Greenhouse Effect

Burning oil, coal, and wood releases carbon dioxide into the air. Carbon dioxide is an insulator. The more carbon dioxide we release into the air, the warmer the planet becomes. Planting trees is a way to absorb the carbon dioxide and allow the planet to become cooler. Try the following experiment with the students: Put about a teaspoon of water in two jars. Put the lid on one of the jars and leave the other one open. Place both of the jars in a sunny spot and let them sit for several hours. When you go back to check on the jars, you will find that the open jar looks about the same as it did originally. However, the closed jar will look hot and steamy inside because the heat caused by the sun had no way to escape.

The Greenhouse Effect and the Oceans

Ask the students if they think the greenhouse effect could cause our oceans to rise. Then, in a 2-cup glass measuring cup, place half of an apple, cut side down. This represents land. Put several ice cubes on top of the apple, then enough water to cover about two-thirds to three-quarters of the apple. After the ice has melted, have students check the level of the water. Is more of the apple covered with water than before? When ice that is on the land, such as glaciers, melts due to excess heat, the water drains into the oceans and the water level rises.

Repeat the experiment without the apple. (This represents icebergs and water.) Have students measure the level of the ice and water. After the ice melts, record the level of the water. Why didn't it change? Water formed when the ice melted and replaced the ice that was under water, so there is no increase in the water level. Would the oceans' water level change if all the icebergs melted? Would the water level change if all the snow and ice in Alaska melted?

More on the Greenhouse Effect

The sun's energy warms the Earth, but some of the energy is naturally lost because the Earth radiates some of the heat back into the atmosphere and out into space. Pollution of our air is trapping this extra heat and causing what is known as the greenhouse effect. Scientists say that this trapping of excess heat is causing the Earth's atmosphere to heat up. To demonstrate this principle to the class, you need three small jars and two thermometers. Place each thermometer in an empty glass jar. Invert the last jar and place it on top of one of the jars containing a thermometer so that the thermometer is enclosed inside the two jars. Place both jar setups in a place where the sun will shine on them equally. After one hour, record the temperatures on both thermometers. The thermometer inside the two jars will register a higher temperature than the thermometer inside the open jar. If you have only one thermometer, set up the two jars as described and, after one hour, remove the top jar and record the temperature on the thermometer. Then let the thermometer sit in the open jar for another hour and record the difference in temperature that results.

Toilet Paper is Not All the Same

How can different types of toilet paper affect our environment? Ask the students to bring in different types of toilet tissue: scented, unscented, colored, white, and single ply and double ply. Have the students place the same amount of each type of tissue into separate, clear jars along with enough water to cover the sheets, then place tight-fitting lids on the jars. The students should shake each container the same length of time every day until all of the contents have decomposed. Have the students predict which types of tissue will decompose first, second, and so forth. Discuss and record your daily observations and compare the results. Ask the students to compare the cost of each brand and the "quality" of each: Which is the best buy financially? Which is the best buy ecologically?

Is It All Garbage?

Set up four containers in your classroom labeled "Reusable," "Recyclable," "Garbage," and "Trash." Discuss what types of items would belong in each of the bins. ("Garbage" would be food products, and "Trash" would be the leftover goods that cannot be reused or recycled.) Have students bring in various items and place them in the proper bins. (You can also have students discard their daily "garbage" in the proper bins.) After several days, have them note what and how many items are discarded in the "Trash" bin. Discuss what they can do to decrease the amount of trash their families and the class generate. Make a list of these possibilities.

Acid Rain

Acid rain, a form of air pollution, is created when fossil fuels are burned. It can be stopped in many ways, such as by using scrubbers, special devices in smokestacks that remove harmful wastes. Ask students to take samples of the rain that falls in your area by placing a plastic cup outside their homes where it will catch rain falling directly from the sky. They should secure the cup by tying it to a railing on a porch or deck or by tying it to a stake in an open spot in the yard. After it rains, ask them to bring the cups to class. Test the acidity of the water by placing wide-range pH strips (available from a scientific supply house, pool supply stores, and some school supply houses) in the samples for a few seconds. The lower the number associated with the color the strip turns, the more acid the rain is. The higher the number, the more basic the water is. After you have tested the rain from several rainfalls, determine whether your area's rainfall is more acidic than you would like it to be. If so, write a class letter to your state representative urging him or her to take steps to eliminate acid rain.

Rusty Liberty

Duplicate the effect that sea air, weather, and pollution have had on the Statue of Liberty with the following experiment:

- You'll need two pennies, salt, plastic wrap, a shallow bowl, vinegar, rubber bands, paper towels, two twist ties, and a fingernail file.
- Fold the paper towel to fit in the bottom of a shallow bowl. Lightly dampen the towel with water and sprinkle a small amount of salt on it. Then add a dash of vinegar.
- Use the fingernail file to scrape off any dirt that is on the edges of the two pennies.
- Take the paper off the two twist ties. Scrape the wires of both ties until they are shiny. Wrap one wire around one of the pennies and wind the other wire up into a coil.
- Put both pennies and the coil of wire on top of the paper towel and cover the bowl with the plastic wrap. Have the students examine the bowl every few hours to see which of the three samples corrodes the quickest. The vinegar on the towel represents the acid in the air from pollution; the salt and water duplicate the saltwater spray that surrounds the Statue of Liberty. The plastic wrap keeps the air humid, as sea air would be. The pennies are like Liberty's copper body, and the wires are her iron parts.

Ask the students if they think the same rate of corrosion would occur if Liberty was made only of iron, or only of copper? Compose a class letter to the governor of New York suggesting that the Statue of Liberty be totally covered with either iron or copper, based on the results of your experiment.

Earth As an Apple

After doing the following demonstration, discuss with your class the importance of taking care of the soil and not polluting or overworking it.

- Slice an apple into quarters. Set three of the quarters aside to represent the world's oceans.
- Cut the remaining quarter, which represents the Earth's land area, in half. Set one of these halves aside. This half represents the land area on Earth that is inhospitable to humans (polar areas, deserts, swamps, high-altitude mountains).
- The portion of the apple that you have left (1/8 of the original apple) represents the land area that people live on. Slice this piece into four sections. Set three of these sections aside. They represent areas too rocky, wet, cold, steep, or populated to grow food.
- Carefully peel the skin off the remaining section (1/32 of the apple). This tiny peel represents the portion of the Earth's surface that is cultivated.

Get Involved

Become involved in your community's efforts to clean up litter. Organize a group of students from your school, church, or neighborhood to do one of the following activities:

- Take a walk along a stream, lake, or river to clean up the trash.

- Contact your local government to see if they sponsor an "adopt a highway" program. If so, volunteer for a section of highway and help clean up the trash.
- Contact the Center for Marine Conservation (see "Additional Resources" at the end of this unit) and request information on their beach clean-up program. Volunteer for this work.

■ Creative Writing Activities

Following are instructions to give the students for various writing activities.

- Write a paper describing how you would make the world more beautiful. The stories will be bound together to make a class book. (*Miss Rumphius* by Cooney)
- In the early days of the pioneers, the water used for drinking was not purified in any way. A glass of drinking water could be brown with visible particles floating around in it. Today, our water is purified before we drink it. Write a futuristic story describing what it would be like if the water in our lakes, rivers, and reservoirs was so polluted that it could not be purified by any known process. How would this affect our daily lives? Would we become used to this as our pioneer ancestors before us did? (*Just a Dream* by Van Allsburg)
- Write out a menu and an itinerary for a family picnic. Concentrate on having as little waste as possible left after your family event.
- Write the scripts for commercials to promote waste reduction in your school or home. Read your commercials in front of the class or at the dinner table and discuss what you as a class or family can do to reduce the amount of waste that is generated in your classroom or home. (*Great Trash Bash* by Leedy)
- Global warming is a subject of interest to many scientists today. Write your own story about how life in your town might change as a consequence of the Earth's temperature becoming progressively warmer. Would there be good consequences of global warming? What areas of your life would this affect?
- Think of ways in which water can become polluted through runoff from rain (e.g., soap used to wash a car; spillage of gasoline when refueling your car; animal wastes; use of poisonous cleaners outdoors). Write a newspaper article informing citizens of a pollution problem that came about simply because normal citizens were not aware of the results of their actions. (*Lake Fear* by McMahan)
- As local rivers and lakes become more and more polluted, scientists are studying cloud seeding, desalinization (removing salt from sea water), and moving icebergs as methods of obtaining new sources of fresh water. Do some research on these different alternatives, then write a report stating your position on which alternative is most viable.
- Your teacher will try to arrange for a member of the Environmental Protection Agency to speak to your group. If this is not possible, then send away for information from the EPA and read and discuss it in class. After discussing the information, write letters to local officials or representatives of factories in the area whose operations cause environmental problems, stating your concerns and asking them to become more active in protecting the environment.
- Look around your house and make a list of all the items that bear the recycling symbol (three arrows in a triangular shape with a number in the middle of the triangle). Check with your parents to determine if these items are actually being recycled. Write an essay about what you found, including your list of products as an attachment to the essay and steps you plan to take to ensure that more items around your home are recycled.
- Read *A Tale of Antarctica* by Glimmerveen. This book focuses on the problems our environment faces because of our "throwaway" society. After reading the book, write down ideas on ways that you can change this throwaway attitude. (You may want to follow up this activity by

discussing "Every Litter Bit Hurts" (#25, page 74, in *50 Simple Things Kids Can Do to Save the Earth* by The Earth Works Group; see section 2, chapter 2).

- Write a paper about something in nature that you are particularly fond of. Explain why you like it so much and discuss the effects pollution could have on it.

- Air pollution is a growing problem in our country and around the world. Write a convincing paragraph to be used as a radio or television advertisement. If done for television, develop a skit to accompany the words. You can also develop a comic strip that relays the importance of curtailing air pollution. (*Song of the Smoggy Stars* by Molarsky)

■ Art Activities

Following are instructions to give the students for various art activities.

- Collect several of the plastic rings used to bind six-packs of soda pop. Glue the rings to a sheet of paper. Inside each of the circles, draw a picture that illustrates an activity that you can participate in to help control pollution. The six pictures can be cartoon-style, cutouts from magazines, or a six-step process to alleviate pollution. (*A Tale of Antarctica* by Glimmerveen)

- Decorate a grocery bag with ecology messages and decorations. Go for a walk with your class and take your ecology bag to collect litter outside. (Only safe items! No glass or objects with sharp edges.) Use the collected litter to make a collage. What will you title your piece of artwork? (*The Wartville Wizard* by Madden)

- Remove the label from a small, empty food container. Remove the lid and clean the can. A can from tuna, cat food, or turkey or chicken chunks will do nicely. (Adult supervision required for younger children.) Put the can on a piece of felt and trace around the bottom of it. Cut out the felt and glue it to the bottom of the can. Trace a circle of the felt that will fit into the inside bottom of the can. Cut out the circle and glue it in place. Cut another strip of the felt to cover the inside edges of the can and glue it in place. Watch for any sharp edges! Decorate the outside of your treasure box with more felt, construction paper, glitter, stickers, or any other material you want. You can use the decorated can to hold jewelry, coins, rocks, or any other treasure you have.

- Make a pencil holder out of an old cardboard tissue roll or a paper towel roll cut in half. Cover the tube with colored paper or wrapping paper and glue it in place. Decorate the tube with any design and materials you want. Make a base for your pencil holder by cutting a circle out of cardboard and covering it with the same color paper that you used on your tube. Or be creative: Use a contrasting color or pattern. Stand your tube up on its end and place the end in the center of the circle. Glue it in place. After the glue has dried, you will have a pencil holder to use or give as a gift. You can also glue three or four tubes of different lengths onto the cardboard and to make holders for pencils, crayons, scissors, and so forth.

- Make a doll out of an old, cleaned-out, 46-ounce frozen juice can and the bottom section of a 2-liter soda pop bottle. After you have cleaned out the juice container, cover it with colored paper and decorate it to represent the body of your doll. You can cover the top third of the container with one color to represent the face and the bottom section in two other colors to represent a shirt or blouse and skirt or pants. Add buttons, bows, belts, and so forth. Make paper arms to glue to each side of the container. Cut the bottom section off a 2-liter bottle of soda. It is usually black but does come in green. Turn this section upside-down and glue it to the top of your doll for a hat. Decorate the hat as you like.

- Make an animal litter bin. Wash out a half-gallon milk carton and staple the opening of the container shut. Cut a 5-by-2 1/2-inch hole in one side of the container. The top inch of the hole should extend into the slanted section at the top of the milk carton. This is your animal's mouth. Decorate the milk carton to resemble the animal of your choice. Poke a hole in each side of the carton toward the top. Feed one end of a piece of yarn or rope through each hole and tie a knot to secure it. Your litter bin is ready to hang up and "eat" trash.

- Make a festive "goodie" basket out of a discarded berry basket from the grocery store. Obtain a berry basket and rinse it out. Cover the outside of the basket with colored tissue paper. Decorate the paper with stickers, glitter, or cutouts. Twist two different-colored pipe cleaners (chenille sticks) together to make the handle of your basket. Poke a small hole in two opposite sides of your basket at the top. Stick one of the handles through each hole and twist the pipe cleaners together to secure them. Fill your basket with candies, cookies, or small gifts and give it to the person of your choice.

- Construct a "model city" out of paper or clay or draw a blueprint, to scale, specifying the number of stories for each building and having a legend. Imagine that the number of people in your city has increased by 25 percent. Increase the number of buildings, parking lots, recreation areas, and so forth, to handle the increased population without enlarging the size (square mileage) of the city. What were the results, physically and aesthetically?

- Make a school or church bus out of a milk carton. Wash out a half-gallon cardboard milk container. Open up the top of the container. Cut down the four side seams of the top so that you can fold the flaps down and close the container. The top of the carton should look identical to the bottom—the container should be the shape of a rectangle. Cover the carton with colored paper and glue it in place. Make windows out of white paper cut into squares or rectangles. Show the people who are riding in the bus through the windows. Use a marker to put any signs that you want on the sides, front, or back of the bus. Cut four tires out of cardboard and color or paint them black. Glue them in place. Use yellow construction paper, circles of aluminum foil, or the caps from two 2-liter bottles for headlights.

- Draw a line down the center of a white piece of paper. On one side of the paper, make a drawing of a nature scene (e.g., a forest with a creek running through it, a lake, the river running past a town). On the other side of the paper, draw the same scene, showing the effects that pollution can have. Present your pictures in front of your class and discuss the effects of pollution and what can be done to reverse them. (*The Lorax* by Geisel)

- Go on a walk around your community and take pictures of places you encounter that are littered. Make a poster, collage, or display showing what you found and develop a theme to urge others to prevent littering in the community. (*The Wartville Wizard* by Madden)

- Make a poster that conveys the dangers of air pollution. Include photographs you have taken of areas close to your home that have poor air quality or draw a picture to get your point across. Include steps that can be taken to help fight pollution in your town.

Additional Resources

■ Experiment Books

Celebrating Earth Day: A Sourcebook of Activities & Experiments, by Robert Gardner (Millbrook Press, 1992)
> Offers activities for learning more about the Earth and how to improve its state.

Crafts from Recyclables: Great Ideas from Throwaways, by Colleen Van Blaricam (St. Martin's Press, 1992).
> Ordinary household items are made into a variety of items by following easy-to-understand directions.

Earth Book for Kids, Activities to Help Heal the Environment, by Linda Schwartz (Learning Works, 1990)
> Fun activities and facts are used to help students become better acquainted with their environment and build a desire to care for the Earth.

Environmental Experiments about Air, by Thomas R. Rybolt and Robert C. Mebam (Enslow, 1993)
> Experiments provide information about the air around us and about pollution, the greenhouse effect, and other problems related to our atmosphere.

Experiments That Explore Acid Rain, by Martin J. Gutnik (Twenty-First Century Books, 1992)
> The scientific method is applied in experiments and discussions about acid rain. This is a well-organized text.

Experiments That Explore Oil Spills, by Martin J. Gutnik (Millbrook Press, 1991)
> Eleven experiments allow students to make the connection between the effects of oil spills and prevention. The interruption of the natural life cycle by spilled oil is stressed.

50 Simple Things Kids Can Do to Recycle, by Earth Works Group (Econo-Clad, 1994).
> Recycling activities to try at home, school, or anywhere. A follow-up to *50 Simple Things Kids Can Do to Save the Earth.*

Great Newspaper Crafts, by F. Virginia Walter (Sterling, 1992).
> Numerous ideas for turning newspapers into gifts, decorations, puppets, mobiles, and games. Contains full-color photographs and diagrams.

Learning and Caring about Our World, by Gayle Bittinger (Warren, 1990).
> Art and language activities, learning games, experiments, and poems focus on the land, air, and water around us.

Projects for a Healthy Planet, by Shar Levine and Allison Grafton (John Wiley & Sons, 1992).
> Simple environmental experiments for kids that explain causes of pollution and the importance of protecting our resources and creating products friendly to the environment.

■ *National Geographic* Articles

Endangered Animals

February 1994—"Sea Turtles in a Race," page 94

November 1993—"The Harlequin Duck, Bird of White Waters," page 116

July 1993—"Saving Siberia's Tigers," page 38

June 1993—"Silence of the Songbirds," page 68

February 1993—"Newborn Panda in the Wild," page 60

November 1992—"Eagles on the Rise," page 42

September 1992—"Dolphins in Crisis," page 2

July 1992—"Mountain Lions," page 38

April 1992—"Captives in the Wild," page 122

January 1992—"Last Refuge of the Monk Seal," page 128

September 1991—"America's Illegal Wildlife Trade," page 106

May 1991—Elephants—"Out of Time, Out of Space," page 2

April 1991—"Falcon Rescue," page 106

Diminishing Resources

September 1993—"New Sensors Eye the Rain Forest," page 118

August 1993—"Untamed Treasure of the Cumberland," page 123

May 1993—"Middle East Water—Critical Resource," page 38

March 1993—"Wellspring of the High Plains," page 80

November 1992—"Maya Heartland Under Siege," page 94

October 1992—"Our Disappearing Wetlands," page 3

May 1992—"India's Wildlife Dilemma," page 2

August 1991—"The Best Idea America Ever Had," page 36

June 1991—"Water and the West: The Colorado River," page 2

Pollution

1993 Special Edition: "Water—The Power, Promise and Turmoil of North America's Fresh Water," page 76

June 1993—"Chesapeake Bay—Hanging in the Balance," page 2

August 1992—"Main-Danube Canal Links Europe's Waterways," page 3

March 1992—"Lake Tahoe—Playing for High Stakes," page 113

February 1992—"Persian Gulf Pollution," page 122

August 1991—"After the Storm," page 2

June 1991—"East Europe's Dark Dawn," page 36

May 1991—"Once and Future Landfills," page 116

■ Agencies and Citizens' Groups

Water Pollution

Adopt-a-Stream Foundation
P.O. Box 5558
Everett, WA 98201

Global Tomorrow Coalition/West
708 Southwest 3rd Ave.
Suite 227
Portland, OR 97204
Plastics in the Ocean

Indiana Department of Education
Office of School Assistance
#229 State House
Indianapolis, IN 46204
outdoor water packets

The National Water Alliance
1225 I St., N.W., Suite 300
Washington, D.C. 20005

Seacoast Anti-Pollution League
Five Market St.
Portsmouth, NH 03801

University of Illinois
122 Mumford
1301 West Gregory Dr.
Urbana, IL 61801
water quality fact sheets

Water Quality Branch
Environment Canada
Ottawa, Ontario KIA OH3

Air Pollution

Air Pollution Control
Bureau of National Affairs, Inc.
1231 25th St., NW
Washington, D.C. 20037

Air Pollution Control Association
P.O. Box 2861
Pittsburgh, PA 15230

Office of Air and Radiation
United States Environmental Protection
Agency
Washington, D.C. 20460

Ozone

Environmental Defense Fund
257 Park Ave., South
New York, NY 10010

Friends of the Earth
218 D. St., S.E.
Washington, D.C. 20003

National Resources Defense Council
40 West 20th St.
New York, NY 10011

Hazardous Waste

Aluminum Association
900 19th St., N.W
Washington, D.C. 20006

American Paper Institute
260 Madison Ave.
New York, NY 10016

Center for Environmental Education
1725 DeSales St., NW Suite 500
Washington, D.C. 20036

Citizens Clearinghouse for Hazardous Waste
P.O. Box 926
Arlington, VA 22216

Columbus Clean Community
181 S. Washington Blvd.
Columbus, OH 43215

Earth Birthday Project
183 Pinehurst No. 34
New York, NY 10033

Environmental Defense Fund
257 Park Ave., South
New York, NY 10010

Kids Against Pollution
Tenakell School
275 High St.
Closter, NJ 07624

National Recycling Coalition
1101 30th St., NW Suite 305
Washington, D.C. 20007

Radioactive Waste Campaign
625 Broadway, Second Floor
New York, NY 10012

Recycling Eco-News
625 Broadway, 2nd Floor
New York, NY 10012

Renew America
1400 Sixteenth St., NW Suite 710
Washington, D.C. 20036

Toxic Avengers
c/o El Puente
211 South Fourth St.
Brooklyn, NY 11211

Washington State Department of Ecology
4350 150th Ave., NE
Redmond, WA 98052

Endangered Animals

Animal Welfare Institute
P.O. Box 3650
Washington, D.C. 20057
Endangered Animals Handbook, available for
educators

Center for Action on Endangered Species
175 West Main St.
Ayer, MA 01432

Defenders of Wildlife
1244 19th St., NW
Washington, D.C. 20036

Endangered Species Office
U.S. Fish & Wildlife Service
18th & C Sts., NW
Washington, D.C. 20240

Greenpeace, U.S.A.
1436 U St., NW
Washington, D.C. 20009
202-462-1177

National Audubon Society
950 Third Ave.
New York, NY 10022
212-832-3200

National Wildlife Federation
1400 16th St., N.W.
Washington, D.C. 20036

RARE, Inc.
1601 Connecticut Ave., NW
Washington, D.C. 20009

Save the Manatee Club
500 N. Maitland Ave. Suite 200
Maitland, FL 32751

Timber Wolf Alliance
Sigurd Olson Environmental Institute
Northland College
Ashland, WI 54806

The Whale Center
3929 Piedmont Ave.
Oakland, CA 94611

Whales Adoption Project
634 N. Falmouth Hwy. Box 388
N. Falmouth, MA 02556

Wilderness Society
900 17th St., NW
Washington, D.C. 20006

Wildlife Conservation International
N.Y. Zoological Society
Bronx, NY 10460

Wildlife Rescue, Inc.
4000 Middlefield Rd. Building V
Palo Alto, CA 94303

World Society for the Protection of Animals
29 Perkins St.
P.O. Box 190
Boston, MA 02130

WWF (World Wildlife Fund)
250 24th St., NW Suite 400
Washington, D.C. 20037
202-293-4800

Environmental

Acid Rain Foundation
1630 Blackhawk Hills
St. Paul, MN 55122

Acid Rain Information Clearinghouse Library
Center for Environmental Information, Inc.
33 S. Washington St.
Rochester, NY 14608

Alliance to Save Energy
1925 K St., NW Suite 206
Washington, D.C. 20036

Canadian Environmental Network
P.O. Box 1289, Station B
Ottawa, Ontario KIP 5R3

Center for Coastal Studies
P.O. Box 1036
Provincetown, MA 02657

Center for Environmental Education
1725 DeSales St., NW Suite 500
Washington, D.C. 20036

Center for Marine Conservation
1725 DeSales St., NW Suite 500
Washington, D.C. 20036

The Children's Rain Forest
P.O. Box 936
Lewiston, MA 04240

Citizens for a Better Environment
942 Market St. Suite 505
San Francisco, CA 94102

Educators for Social Responsibility
23 Garden St.
Cambridge, MA 02138

Environmental Action Coalition
625 Broadway
New York, NY 10012

Environmental Defense Fund
257 Park Ave., South
New York, NY 10010
212-505-2100

Greenpeace
1436 U St., NW
Washington, D.C. 20009
202-462-1177

The Institute for Earth Education
P.O. Box 288
Warrenville, IL 60555

The Institute for Environmental Education
32000 Chagrin Blvd.
Cleveland, OH 44124

Keep America Beautiful
9 West Broad St.
Stamford, CT 06892

Kids for a Clean Environment
P.O. Box 158254
Nashville, TN 37215
800-952-3223

National Association for Humane &
Environmental Education
67 Salem Rd.
East Haddam, CT 06423-0362
KIND News, leaflets, posters

National Energy Foundation
Resources for Education
National Office
5160 Wiley Post Way Suite 200
Salt Lake City, UT 84116

The Nature Conservancy
1815 N. Lynn St.
Arlington, VA 22209

Pollution Probe
12 Madison Ave.
Toronto, Ontario M5R 2S1

Rain Forest Action Network
301 Broadway, Suite A
San Francisco, CA 94133

Sierra Club
730 Polk St.
San Francisco, CA 94109
415-776-2211

United Nations Environment Programs
North American Office
Room DC2-0803 United Nations
New York, NY 10017

Washington State Department of Ecology
Litter Control & Recycling Program
4350 150th Ave., NE
Redmond, WA 98052

■ Magazines

The Dolphin Log
Cousteau Society
870 Greenbrier Cir. Suite 402
Chesapeake, VA 23320
804-523-9335

■ Videos/Films

Garbage Tale: An Environmental Adventure (Churchill Films, 1990). Upper level. 18 mins. Available for purchase in video or film.

     A fantasy about a young boy who learns about waste problems through a singing and dancing trash collector.

Recycling: Waste Into Wealth (Bullfrog Films, 1985). Upper level. 28 mins. Available to rent or purchase in video or film.

Documentary on Portland, Oregon, families who recycle their trash regularly. Tells how to implement a recycling program locally.

Recycling Is Fun! (Bullfrog Films, 1991). P, I levels. 12 mins. Available to rent or purchase in video or film.

Three children visit a landfill, a recycling center, and a supermarket to learn about ways they can help their world.

Reducing, Reusing, and Recycling: Environmental Concerns. (Rainbow Educational Video, 1990). I, U levels. 22 mins. Video available for purchase.

Achievable goals for families to protect their environment through everyday activities.

Save the Earth: A How-To Video (International Video Publications, 1990). Upper level. 60 mins. Video available for purchase in association with "Save the Earth Brigade."

Save the Earth Brigade gives practical ideas for reusing, recycling, and reducing in a nicely produced, inexpensive, upbeat video.

Producers of Films and Videos

Arthur Mokin Publications, Inc.
P.O. Box 1866
Santa Rosa, CA 95402
Disappearance of the Great Rain Forest,
for rent or purchase

National Geographic Society
Educational Services
Department 89
Washington, D.C. 20036
Exploring Ecology

■ Web Sites

The following Web sites will reference additional Web sites relating to ecology. These Web sites were created especially for children. All sites were accessed in March 2001 and were active at that time.

Recycling: http://www.yahooligans.com/science_and_oddities/Earth_the/Environment/Recycling

The following Web sites discuss specific topics related to the environment and ecology:

http://www.yahooligans.com/science_and_nature/Earth_the/Environment/

Conservation organizations: http://www.yahooligans.com/science_and_oddities/Earth_the/Environment/Conservation_Organizations

Earth Day: http://www.yahooligans.com/science_and_oddities/Earth_the/Environment/Earth_Day

Global warming: http://www.yahooligans.com/science_and_oddities/Earth_the/Environment/Global_warming

Acid rain: http://www.epa.gov/

Composting: http://aggie-horticulture.tamu.edu/extension/compost/chapter7.html

Earthwatch Organization: http://www.earthwatch.org/

Endangered species: http://www.fws.gov/

EPA—Acid rain: http://www.epa.gov/airmarkets/acidrain/

Greenhouse effect: http://kaos.erin.gov.au/air/

Making Paper: http://www.inveresk.co.uk/mkrecyc.html
National Wildlife Federation: http://www.igc.apc.org/
Recycling: http://www.fmc.sc.edu/recycle/Educate.html
World Wildlife Fund: http://www.wwf.org/

THE WEATHER

Key Concepts

■ Primary Concepts

Students will be able to:

1. Observe, describe, and predict changes in day and night and the seasons (Chapter 1).

2. Identify and find evidence of air as matter (Chapter 2).

    Understand that air has no color, smell, or taste but takes up space.

    Observe how air moves things.

    Recognize that weather occurs in the air.

    Appreciate that all living things need to breathe clean air to stay healthy.

    Understand that they, as members of society, have a responsibility in helping to keep air clean.

3. Identify forms of precipitation (Chapter 3).

4. Explain how a cloud is formed and compare types of clouds (Chapter 3).

5. Observe, describe, and predict changes in weather and cloud cover. Demonstrate ability to chart these observations (all chapters).

■ Intermediate Concepts

Students will be able to:

1. Define and describe the basic kinds of air masses (Chapter 2).

2. Describe conditions that occur when a warm front meets a cold front (Chapter 2).

3. Explain the causes of wind and how wind speed is measured and describe the various instruments used (barometer, anemometer, wind vane) (Chapter 2).

4. Describe what a meteorologist does and list reasons why this occupation is important to society (Chapter 2).

5. Explain what a weather forecast is and recognize basic forecasting symbols (Chapter 2).

6. Explain evaporation and condensation and diagram the water cycle (Chapter 3).

7. Describe the atmospheric conditions necessary to cause precipitation (rain, snow, sleet, and hail) and, given a set of conditions, predict the type of precipitation that would occur (Chapter 3).

8. Identify various types of clouds, describe the weather conditions that cause them, and indicate the different types of precipitation produced by each (Chapter 3).

9. Describe the weather conditions associated with different storms (thunderstorms, tornadoes, and hurricanes) (Chapter 3).

10. Identify conditions that make up weather. List and describe factors that influence weather (all chapters).

■ Upper Concepts

Students will be able to:

1. Explain the different rates at which energy from the sun is absorbed by the land and water (Chapter 1).

2. Explain the cause of the seasons (Chapter 1).

3. Define air pressure, discuss why air pressure varies within the atmosphere, and describe the relationship between air pressure and wind (Chapter 2).

4. Define the types of weather fronts and describe the formation of each (Chapter 2).

5. Explain how the unequal heating of the air and the force of gravity produce convection circulation in the atmosphere (Chapter 2).

6. Describe the information required by a meteorologist to predict weather conditions (Chapter 2).

7. Identify five meteorological instruments and indicate the information provided through the use of each (Chapter 2).

8. Differentiate between an aneroid and a mercurial barometer and know how to use each to measure air pressure (Chapter 2).

9. Discuss the causal factors of destructive weather conditions (thunderstorms, tornadoes, hurricanes) (Chapter 3).

10. Gather weather data over a designated period, analyze the data, and predict the weather conditions that may be expected to occur (Chapters 2, 3).

Comprehensive Teaching Resources

The following table lists books that cover a wide range of topics about weather. One of these books could serve as your main teaching guide while studying this unit. Each book is listed with a short summary, and the chapters in this book that it applies to are noted. The books are listed by degree of difficulty, easiest to most difficult.

BOOK AND SUMMARY	AUTHOR	CHAPTERS		
		1	2	3
Air, Water, and Weather (Facts on File, 1987) Explains the elements of weather and how they interact to create different weather patterns.	Michael Pollard		X	X
Junior Science Weather (Gloucester Press, 1988) Learn about fog, rain, snow, and wind. Contains many experiments: make a rain gauge, a temperature chart, and a windsock.	Terry Jennings		X	X
Our World Weather & Climate (Silver Burdett, 1991) An overview of weather: atmosphere, wind, clouds and rain, storms, and climate.	John Mason		X	X
Read About Weather (Raintree Children's Books, 1988) An introduction to weather, discussing evaporation/condensation, clouds, rain, snow, thunderstorms, and hurricanes.	Herta S. Breiter		X	X
Weather (Franklin Watts, 1994) Easy-to-understand explanation of precipitation, wind, clouds, thunder, and lightning. Also discusses the effects of pollution.	Martyn Bramwell		X	X
Weather Forecasting (Macmillan, 1987) Describes forecasters at work using equipment to track the changing weather. Cartoon-style drawings.	Gail Gibbons	X	X	X

Each chapter in this section lists reference books that focus on the specific area of the weather being addressed. These books can be used to complement and expand upon the basic information provided in the comprehensive resource books listed in the previous table.

The reference books in each chapter have been classified by age level to help you select those that best fit the needs and interests of your student(s).

Chapter 1

The Sun and the Seasons

■ Teaching Resources

Books containing experiment(s) relating to the subject matter are marked with a plus sign (+) before and after the title.

P   +*Autumn Days,*+ by Ann Schweninger (Puffin Books, 1993)
The arrival of a new season brings exciting changes in the landscape and hard-to-answer questions from small children. This book answers these questions and provides a good description of what autumn is.

P   *Changing Seasons: Walkabout,* by Henry Pluckrose (Children's Press, 1994)
Simple text and beautiful illustrations explain the differences in the seasons.

P   *How Do You Know It's Fall?,* by Allan Fowler (Children's Press, 1992)
Two books with simple text and beautiful photographs depict the characteristics of fall.

P   *How Do You Know It's Spring?,* by Allan Fowler (Children's Press, 1991)
Two books with simple text and beautiful photographs depict the characteristics of spring.

P   *How Do You Know It's Summer?,* by Allan Fowler (Children's Press, 1992).
Two books with simple text and beautiful photographs depict the characteristics of summer.

P   *How Do You Know It's Winter?,* by Allan Fowler (Children's Press,1991)
Two books with simple text and beautiful photographs depict the characteristics of winter.

P   *Pond Year,* by Kathryn Lasky (Econo-Clad, 1999)
Two young girls learn that the life and uses of a pond change with the seasons.

P   +*Spring,*+ by Ruth Thomson and Sally Hewitt (Children's Press, 1994)
An introduction describing why spring exists, followed by craft and science projects that tie in. (Also available are *Summer, Autumn,* and *Winter,* 1994.)

P   *Sun Up, Sun Down,* by Gail Gibbons (Harcourt Brace Jovanovich, 1987)
Describes the characteristics of the sun and the ways in which it regulates life on Earth. Has bold, colorful illustrations and easy text.

P/I *The Reasons for Seasons,* by Gail Gibbons (Holiday House, 1995)
Author explains why and how the seasons happen.

P/I +*Sunshine Makes the Seasons,*+ by Franklyn M. Branley (Thomas Y. Crowell, 1985)
Describes how sunshine and the tilt of the Earth's axis are responsible for the changing seasons.

I *How Leaves Change,* by Sylvia A. Johnson (Lerner, 1986)
Describes how leaves change as a natural part of the cycle of the seasons.

I *The Sun,* by Seymour Simon (Econo-Clad, 1999)
Describes the nature of the sun, its origin, source of energy, layers, atmosphere, sunspots, and activity.

I *Weatherwise: Learning about the Weather,* by Jean M. Craig (Jonathon D. Kahl, 1992)
Discusses many aspects of the weather, including climate and the seasons, wind, humidity, clouds, rain, and weather forecasting.

■ Reading Selections

Books marked with an asterisk (*) before and after the title are related to activities in the activity sections of this chapter.

Animal Seasons, by Brian Wildsmith (Oxford University Press, 1991)
> Follows what happens to different animals with each change of seasons.

Autumn Harvest, by Alvin Tresselt (Lothrop, Lee & Shepard, 1951)
> A journey through a country town during autumn and harvest time.

Dakota Dugout, by Ann Turner (Econo-Clad, 1999)
> A woman describes her experiences living with her husband on the Dakota prairie and the effects of the seasons on their lives.

Do You Know What I'll Do?, by Charlotte Zolotow (HarperCollins Juvenile Books, 2000)
> A story of the seasons and the holidays from a child's point of view.

The Hot and Cold Summer, by Johanna Hurwitz (Scholastic, 1991)
> Two inseparable 10-year-old boys discover there is room in their friendship for another person, and it really doesn't matter that she is a girl.

A New Coat for Anna, by Harriet Ziefert (Alfred A. Knopf, 1986)
> Even though there is no money, Anna's mother finds a way to make her a badly needed new coat for winter.

Ox Cart Man, by Donald Hall (Puffin Books, 1979)
> Describes the life of a nineteenth-century New England family throughout the seasons.

The Seasons of Arnold's Apple Tree, by Gail Gibbons (Econo-Clad, 1999)
> As seasons pass, Arnold enjoys a variety of activities as a result of his apple tree. Has a recipe for apple pie and a description of how a cider press works.

The Sun's Asleep Behind the Hill, by Mirra Ginsburg (William Morrow, 1982)
> The sun, the breeze, the leaves, the bird, the squirrel, and the child all grow tired after a long day and go to sleep. This book has large text, few words, and beautiful illustrations.

This Year's Garden, by Cynthia Rylant (Econo-Clad, 1999)
> Follows the seasons of the year through the growth, life, and death of a rural family's garden.

Three Dog Winter, by Elizabeth Van Steenwyk (Yearling Books, 1999)
> The world of sled dog racing in northern Montana forms the background for a 12-year-old boy's adjustment to his father's death, his mother's remarriage, and the integration of two families into one. (Chapter Book)

Winter Holding Spring, by Crescent Dragonwagon (Atheneum, 1990)

> In discussing her mother's death with her father, 11-year-old Sarah comes to see that endings provide beginnings; in winter there is a promise of spring. (Chapter Book)

A Winter Journey, by David Updike (Prentice-Hall, 1985)

> Homer goes out at night into a snowstorm in search of his dog, Sophocles, and experiences some strange and thrilling adventures. Contains colorful illustrations. (Also available are *An Autumn Tale* (Pippin Press, 1988) and *The Sounds of Summer* (Pippin Press, 1993)).

Winter Poems, by Barbara Rogasky (Scholastic, 1999)

> A collection of poems about the seasons, ranging from late fall to early spring, by authors such as Edgar Allan Poe, William Shakespeare, Emily Dickinson, and Robert Frost.

Winter Woods, by David Spohn (Lothrop, Lee & Shepard, 1991)

> A boy and his father go out to chop firewood and enjoy the winter environment around them.

A Year of Beasts, by Ashley Wolff (E. P. Dutton, 1986)

> Chronicles the seasons month by month and shows which creatures come out with each new month.

The following books are out of print, but may be available at the local library.

First Comes Spring, by Anne Rockwell (Thomas Y. Crowell, 1985)

> A bear child notices that the clothes he wears, the things everyone does at work and play, and other parts of his world all change with the seasons.

The Four Seasons of Brambly Hedge, by Jill Barklem (Philomel Books, 1990)

> Four short stories about the four seasons as they are spent by the occupants of Brambly Hedge.

My Favorite Time of Year, by Susan Pearson (Harper & Row, 1988)

> A little girl tries to determine what her favorite time of year is.

On a Hot, Hot Day, by Nicki Weiss (G. P. Putnam, 1992)

> A mother and young son enjoy activities together during each season of the year.

The Sun's Day, by Mordicai Gerstein (Harper & Row, 1989)

> An hour-by-hour description of the activities that take place as the sun rises, moves through the sky, and finally sets. Book has large print and few words.

Sun's Up, by Teryl Euvremer (Crown, 1987)

> The sun rises from its bed in the morning, spends the day moving across the sky while engaged in different activities, and then goes to sleep as night falls. This book contains no words; only illustrations.

Tattercoats, by Bernadette Watts (North-South Books, 1988)

> A once-proud scarecrow becomes bedraggled as he is neglected during the winter.

Under Your Feet, by Joanne Ryder (Four Winds Press, 1990)

> Contains poems about nature and wildlife through all of the seasons.

■ Science Activities

The Sun and Climates

Discuss with the class where on Earth it is warmest and coldest. Have the students look on a globe or a world map and locate the equator and areas where the weather would be warm. Then have them identify the areas where it would be coldest and guess why. For more detail, have the students look at the climate near the equator. All areas are all warm, but are they all the same? Compare and contrast the climates of Nairobi, Kenya, and Belem, Brazil. Advanced students may pursue how the economy of a country depends on the climate. Ask them to identify the natural resources and major exports of Alaska, Brazil, Iceland, Mexico, Greenland, Australia, Egypt, and other countries.

The Sun and Shadows

Have the students trace the shadow of an object on a piece of paper in the morning and again at noon. Ask them: How does the shadow change? What do you predict the shadow will look like in the afternoon? Why? As a follow-up, children can place objects in different parts of the yard and trace the shadow, then see if the other children (or you) can guess what the object was. Have the students compare the object's shadow when it is drawn at different times of the day.

Weather's Influence in History

Discuss how the weather could have affected important historical events. Ask the students to speculate about how different weather conditions could have changed history. Events that could be discussed include:

Christopher Columbus's trip to the New World

The settling of Jamestown; other New World settlements

Valley Forge during the Revolutionary War

Adolf Hitler's attack on Russia in World War II

The assassination of President John Kennedy

■ Weather When Traveling

Pick a season and plan a class trip to a special spot. Have the students use a road map to plan the route. They should look up the average temperature of the location and determine what type of clothing and recreational equipment they will need. Discuss what the weather will be at their destination (that is, plan a trip from a cold location to a warm one, or vice versa). Advanced students can calculate the cost of the trip.

The Seasons' Effects on Our Bodies

Discuss how our bodies react to changing temperatures during the different seasons. Ask students what precautions they would take to protect their bodies in extreme weather.

The Seasons' Effects on an Apple Tree

Read *The Seasons of Arnold's Apple Tree* by Gibbons. In the book, there is a recipe for an apple pie that you can bake. Use this as an opportunity to practice math skills.

• Let the students measure and pour the ingredients.

- Weigh the apples. Ask the students what they think the apple slices will weigh after they are peeled and the cores are removed. Have them calculate what percent of the apples will be baked in the pie.
- Ask the students what the diameter and circumference of the pie pan are and what the area of a pie crust with that diameter would be.
- Have the students guess how the measurements would change if they wanted to double, triple, or halve the recipe.

Changing Temperatures

Chart the high and low temperatures in your city for a week. Compare these to average highs and lows for each of the other seasons. Discuss with the students why the temperatures in each season are different. Have them look on the globe and guess which cities might have similar temperatures to their city, then look up these cities and see if they were right.

The Holiday Season

We tend to think about a holiday in terms of how we celebrate it in our homes and in our particular climate; however, climates differ. It is not always cold and snowy at Christmas and Thanksgiving. Also, summer is not hot and sunny in all places on Earth. Have the students choose cities around the globe that experience weather different than yours and investigate what the weather is like there in the different seasons and on the different holidays. They should list seasonal activities that take place in each of the cities and indicate whether they are the same or differ because the weather is different. Have the students list ways in which various people in these cities celebrate holidays and explain whether their customs differ from each other. Ask them whether any differences are due to the differences in the weather.

■ Creative Writing Activities

Following are instructions to give the students for various writing activities.

- Write a story about a time when it was so hot that you wished the sun would stop shining.
- Write words to accompany the illustrations of a wordless book about the sun rising and setting. (*Sun's Up* by Euvremer)
- Write a story about the animals in your area and what their habits are during the season you are experiencing now.
- Do you enjoy the climate you live in, or would you prefer a region with longer summers, longer winters, no winters, and so forth? Write a persuasive argument for staying in your town or for moving away.
- What is your favorite holiday? During what season does it occur? Describe the weather and how it adds to or detracts from the joy of the holiday.
- Read *Tattercoats* by Watts. Write a new ending for the story. What new adventures lie ahead for the scarecrow?
- Re-create an event from the past (either your own past or an event from history). Rewrite the story to have the event take place in a different season than it actually did. For example, imagine your family Christmas happening in weather opposite to what you are used to, rewrite your favorite vacation to the beach taking place in a huge snow storm, or take a skiing trip where the temperature ends up being warm and mild.

- Write a story about a time that you went walking in the woods after a snowfall. What did you see in the woods? How did it make you feel? Were you alone, or did someone special walk with you?

- Write a letter to a new pen pal about four activities you love to participate in, one for each season of the year.

- You are the owner of the Four Seasons restaurant. Make an insert for a menu describing your "specialty of the house," which changes for each season. What would your specialties be? Illustrate the dishes you invent. (*The Four Seasons of Brambly Hedge* by Barklem)

- How do the seasons affect your responsibilities at home? What jobs do you or your parents do that change according to the season? What duties stay the same throughout the year? Pretend that you are in charge of the yard work at your house. Prepare a quarterly, itemized bill listing the work that you performed outdoors and the fee that you would charge for your services.

- Write a letter to a friend describing a day at the beach. What was the weather like? What did you do at the beach? Who went with you?

- It is often said that, "April showers bring May flowers." Write about a time when the month of April was very dry and no flowers bloomed in May. How did this change spring that year? Did it affect people's moods?

- Write a story about a villain who wants to steal the sun as part of a sinister plot. Why does your villain want the sun? How does he take it? Who is the hero of your story? Does the hero retrieve the missing sun and return it to the world?

- If you could have the perfect weather, what would you choose? Would there be different seasons, or would the weather always be the same? Write a poem describing what "perfect" weather would be for you. Be sure to explain why.

- Read *Winter Poems* by Rogasky. Write a poem for each season and illustrate it. Your teacher will compile the poems and create four separate poetry books; one for each season.

■ Art Activities

Following are instructions to give the students for various art activities.

- Look at a picture from a book or magazine. Draw it as it would appear in another season.

- Study "warm" colors (red, orange, yellow). Paint a picture using warm colors. (Younger children may fingerpaint.)

- Draw a picture of an object, giving it human features. Show the object being used for one of its normal daily activities. (*Sun's Up* by Euvremer)

- Divide a piece of paper into four sections, then draw pictures on it of how you dress during each season.

- Draw or color a picture of what the sun sees outside today at your house. Don't forget to tell what time of day it is. (In a classroom setting, a big book can be made, with students each illustrating a different hour of the day.) (*The Sun's Day* by Gerstein)

- Make a simple "costume" out of construction paper depicting the sun, flowers, clouds, and so forth (or use paper plates with Popsicle stick handles to make masks or puppets). Put on a little play with your classmates showing how the sun helps things grow.

- Design your own winter coat. What color would it be? What material would it be made of? How would it close? Would it have any designs or special features on it? (*A New Coat for Anna* by Ziefert)

- Draw a picture of your favorite summer activity. On the back of the paper, make a picture of your favorite winter activity. Are there any activities that you can enjoy doing in both seasons? Make a separate picture showing these activities. (*On a Hot, Hot Day* by Weiss)

- Draw a picture of what you think Mother Nature would look like. Pretend that Mother Nature has four children, one in charge of each season. Draw a picture of the entire "Nature" family and give each of the children an appropriate name (e.g., King Spring, Susie Summer) and outfit.

- Choose an animal and draw four pictures that depict what that animal does in each of the four seasons. Good animals to use are a bear, a duck, a squirrel, or a monarch butterfly. After everyone is done drawing, the teacher will glue the pictures onto poster board or chart paper; one poster for each season. You will have a collection of animals that you can see change from season to season.

Chapter 2
Air, Temperature, and Wind

■ Teaching Resources

Books containing experiment(s) relating to the subject matter are marked with a plus sign (+) before and after the title.

P   +*Air Is All Around You,*+ by Franklyn M. Branley (Thomas Y. Crowell, 1986)
Describes various properties of air and shows how to prove that air takes up space and that there is air dissolved in water.

P   *Feel the Wind,* by Arthur Dorros (Econo-Clad, 1999)
Explains what causes wind and how it affects our environment. Book contains easy text and colorful illustrations.

P   *Weather Words and What They Mean,* by Gail Gibbons (Holiday House, 1992)
Introduces and defines basic weather terms and concepts.

P   *What Makes the Wind?*, by Laurence Santrey (Troll, 1989)
Describes different types of wind and the effects they can have on Earth. Very little description or detail is given. No photographs.

P   *What's the Weather Today?*, by Allan Fowler (Children's Press, 1991)
A simple explanation of weather and climate.

P/I *Questions and Answers about Weather,* by Jean M. Craig (Scholastic, 1996)
Answers questions about wind, heat, rain, and snow, and looks at weather forecasting methods.

P/I *Weather Everywhere,* by Denise Casey (Macmillan Books for Young Readers, 1995)
Introduction to temperature, wind, and moisture, the three primary elements that create weather conditions.

I   *Weather and Climate* (Time-Life, 1992)
Questions-and-answer format describes the forces involved in the world's weather and climate.

I/U *Temperature,* by Brenda Walpole (Gareth Stevens, 1995)
Discusses elements of temperature such as sunlight and thermometers, water and insulation; examines ways of measuring temperature.

I/U *What Will the Weather Be?*, by Lynda DeWitt (Econo-Clad, 1999)
Explains basic characteristics of weather: temperature, humidity, wind speed, air pressure, and how meteorologists gather data.

U   *Changes in the Wind,* by Margery Facklam (Harcourt Brace Jovanovich, 1986)
Examines factors causing changes in the Earth's climate: ocean currents, rain forests, and the greenhouse effect.

■ Reading Selections

Books marked with an asterisk (*) before and after the title are related to activities in the activity sections of this chapter.

At the Back of the North Wind, by George MacDonald (Tor Books, 1998)
> Diamond, a young boy living in nineteenth-century London, has many adventures as he travels with the beautiful lady North Wind and comes to know the many facets of her protective and violent temper. (Chapter Book)

Earthmaker's Tales: North American Indian Stories about Earth Happenings, by Gretchen Mayo (Walker, 1991)
> A collection of Indian legends about the origin of thunder, tornadoes, and other weather phenomena.

The Emperor and the Kite, by Jane Yolen (Econo-Clad, 1999)
> An emperor imprisoned in a high tower is saved by his daughter and her kite.

The Flyaway Pantaloons, by Joseph Sharples (Carolrhoda Books, 1990)
> The energy of the wind carries a pair of pantaloons on a humorous journey.

Heat Wave at Mud Flat, by James Stevenson (Greenwillow Books, 1997)
> The animals of Mud Flat pay Raymond the Rainmaker to bring relief from the hot weather. Raymond fails, but eventually the rains come anyway.

Hot Air Henry, by Mary Cahoun (William Morrow), 1984
> A sassy Siamese cat stows away on a hot-air balloon and ends up taking a fur-raising flight across the mountains.

Mike's Kite, by Elizabeth MacDonald (Orchard Books, 1990)
> Mike's kite blows away on a windy day, taking him and the people who try to help him with it.

Mirandy and Brother Wind, by Patricia C. McKissack (Econo-Clad, 1999)
> To win first prize in the Junior Cakewalk, Mirandy tries to capture the wind for her partner.

Sailing with the Wind, by Thomas Locker (Dial Books for Young Readers, 1993)
> A young girl discovers the ocean's majestic character when she joins her uncle on a sailing trip.

The Twenty-One Balloons, by William Du Bois (Viking, 1986)
> A wonderful adventure about Professor Sherman, who takes a one-year vacation in a hot-air balloon. (Chapter Book)

Weather or Not: Riddles for Rain and Shine, by Rick Walton (Lerner, 1990)
> A collection of riddles about the weather.

When the Wind Stops, by Charlotte Zolotow (Harper & Row, 1995)
> A mother answers questions about the sun, wind, and seas.

The Wind Blew, by Pat Hutchins (Aladdin, 1993)
> The wind snatches up items from everyone and replaces them in a humorous manner.

Windcatcher, by Avi (Econo-Clad, 1999)

> While learning to sail during a visit to his grandmother's at the Connecticut shore, 11-year-old Tony becomes excited about the rumors of sunken treasure in the area and starts following a couple who seem to be making a mysterious search for something. (Chapter Book)

The following books are out of print, but may be available at the local library.

Earth Weather as Explained by Professor Xargle, by Jeanne Willis (Dutton Children's Books, 1993)

> The extraterrestrial, Professor Xargle, tries to explain the human behavior that accompanies different weather conditions.

The Girl Who Loved the Wind, by Jane Yolen (Harper & Row, 1972)

> Adventures of a young girl in India who can talk to the wind.

Half Chicken, by Alma Flor Ada (Doubleday Books for Young Readers, 1995)

> A Mexican folk tale that explains why weather vanes have a rooster on top of them.

Peter and the North Wind, by Freya Littledale (Scholastic, 1988)

> Peter visits the North Wind, which has blown away his flour and receives in return some magic items whose magic has been sabotaged by an innkeeper.

The Same Wind, by Bette Killion (HarperCollins, 1992)

> A little girl asks the wind that is blowing her curtains if he is the same wind that can sail a boat or form a tornado.

The Turnaround Wind, by Arnold Lobel (Harper & Row, 1988)

> The reader turns the book upside down to see what happens when a fierce wind blows through a country town one afternoon, affecting many different people and animals out enjoying the summer air.

The Very Windy Day, by Elizabeth MacDonald (William Morrow, 1992)

> Four people running errands on a very wind day have their possessions blown away and ultimately returned to them.

Weather Report: Poems, by Jane Yolen (St. Martin's Press, 1993)

> Fifty-two poems about different aspects of the weather.

Willie Bear and the Wish Fish, by Debi Gliori (Macmillan Books for Young Readers, 1995)

> Because Bear Family is always complaining about the weather, a Wish Fish gives them their wishes, and they get more than they bargained for.

The Windchild, by Cheryl Harness (Henry Holt, 1991)

> When Tom accidentally fells with an arrow a girl who turns out to be the Windchild, the wind ceases to blow in the village of Finn.

Windy Day, by Caroline Feller Bauer (Lippincott, 1988)

> A collection of stories and poems about wind by a variety of authors. Book contains a bibliography, a glossary of names for the wind, and a few activities.

■ Science Activities

Heat Intensity

Do this experiment as a demonstration for the students. Place a candle in the middle of a table and light it. Put your hand close to the flame (using caution, of course) and move it slowly back. Describe the difference in heat intensity. Discuss the Earth's distance from the sun and how powerful the sun must be to be able to warm the Earth from such a distance.

Comparing Temperatures

Have students record the temperature highs and lows for a week and determine the average high and low temperature for that period. Older students can make a graph of the data gathered. Discuss what kind of weather followed the highs and the lows. What pattern develops?

Conserving Energy at Home

Ask students to go to the doors and windows of their houses to see if they can feel a draft where air is entering. Have them determine how the air is coming in and recommend some ways to prevent these drafts. Ask them how a draft can affect the amount of energy a furnace uses.

Wind and the Weather

As a class, watch the noon weather forecast, check the Internet, or skim the newspaper for weather information. Have students record the wind velocity and direction, air quality index (if given), and temperature. Discuss what kind of day these numbers represent. Ask students: Why is it important to record wind speed? At what speed does the wind pose a danger? At what index does air quality pose a threat?

Observing Wind Velocity

Place a lit candle on the center of a table. Breathe on the candle, then blow from far away, then move closer and blow. Ask the students to describe what happens to the flame, and why. Have them research the ways in which different wind speeds can affect our environment.

Let's Go Fly a Kite

Have students build kites of their own design (see the kite activity in "Art Activities" in this chapter) or use a kit from the store. One kit could be used as a pattern to make several kites, which children could then decorate to their own specifications. Let children decide what they will use for the tails of their kites. Take the class outside and see if the kites will actually fly. Discuss how kites fly. Older students can try different shapes to see which fly best. Then discuss with them what makes a good kite design.

Sailboat Race

Have students make boats using bars of soap that float. They can construct sails out of paper and toothpicks. Then hold a sailboat race. At the start of the race, have students "create" the needed wind. Discuss the different methods the students used to do this. Which were most effective?

The Existence of Air

Have each student design his or her own experiment to demonstrate that air exists, then perform the experiment and document what happens. Did the experiment get the desired results? Refer to one of the experiment books listed earlier in this chapter for ideas, if needed. (Be sure to use the scientific method when planning your activities.) Show the students the following example of such an experiment: Cover the mouth of a pop bottle with a balloon. Tuck the balloon into the bottle. Blow into the bottle and try to inflate the balloon inside the bottle. Why won't it inflate? (There's already air inside the bottle and no more room for the air you are blowing into the balloon.)

Air Pressure 1

Demonstrate air pressure to the class using the following experiment:
- Materials needed: shallow bowl, birthday candle, 1/2 cup water, empty glass jar, and modeling clay.
- Pour the water into the shallow bowl. Press a small dab of modeling clay in the middle of the bowl so that it sticks to the bottom of it. Stick the birthday candle into the middle of the clay so that it stands upright. Light the candle.
- Place the jar, upside-down, over the candle so that it rests on the bowl and stands on its own. The candle will go out, and the water will be sucked up into the jar.
- When the experiment is completely set up (after the first two steps), the air pressure inside the jar and outside the jar are the same. As the flame from the candle warms up the air inside the jar, the air expands so that there is not enough room inside the jar to hold it. Some of the air exits out of the opening in the jar.
- When the candle is extinguished, the air inside the jar cools and contracts. The air takes up less space inside the jar, so there is less air and air pressure. The pressure outside the jar is greater than the pressure inside the jar. The air pressure outside pushes the water up into the jar.

Air Pressure 2

Have a student blow up a balloon and then release it. Ask the class: What happens to the balloon? Why does it propel itself around the room? What happens when you insert a four-holed button in the opening after you blow up the balloon and let it go? (The air release is much more controlled.)

That's Strong Air!

Have four students blow up one large balloon each. Place a large piece of plywood or any large, flat surface on top of the balloons. Ask the class to predict how many people can sit on the plywood before the balloons pop. (*Note:* It is important to distribute the weight on the plywood as evenly as possible.) Have students carefully sit on the board until the balloons pop. How many people did it take before the balloons popped? Ask the students to explain why. Tell them that air pressure can be used to raise a chair at the beauty parlor or barbershop, and mechanics can use it to jack up a car. Ask them if they can think of other examples of uses of air pressure in daily life.

■ Creative Writing Activities

Following are instructions to give the students for various writing activities.
- Describe a time when the wind played tricks on you. (*The Wind Blew* by Hutchins)

When did a change in weather or temperature ruin a special day for you? What could you have done to make the situation better?
- Some animals prefer cold weather, while others prefer warm weather (e.g., a polar bear versus a brown bear). Pick an animal you'd like to be and tell what type of environment it is best suited to. Write a story about your life as that animal.

- If you could talk to the wind, what would you say? Write a letter to the wind and make a special request. (*The Girl Who Loved the Wind* by Yolen)
- Write a poem about the wind. (*Windy Day* by Bauer)
- Write a story personifying yourself as the wind or the sun. What would you do to change the world around you?
- Write a story about taking a trip in a hot-air balloon. Where did you go and what did you see?
- Pretend that you are living in the future, and you can control the weather. Look at a map. How would you change the weather in different areas? What effects would this produce (good and bad) on the world? Write a persuasive argument for changing the weather in a particular country or city.
- Watch the weather forecast on your local television station for several days. Write your own weather forecast telling what the weather will be like for the next day and forecasting what the temperature will be for the next several days of the week. Check your forecast against the actual weather for those days.
- A person who talks all the time without taking time to listen to what others have to say is sometimes said to be "full of hot air." Write a story in which the lead character is such a person, who ends up getting into quite a bit of difficulty because he or she thinks they "know it all." Create a hero for the story who finally succeeds in making your lead character see his or her mistake.

■ Art Activities

Following are instructions to give the students for various art activities.

- Using hollow tubes (from wrapping paper, paper towels, or toilet paper), try to make sounds like the wind howling. What other items can you find to make "windy" sounds? Try attaching small pieces of wax paper to the end of the tube with a rubber band and describe how that sounds.
- Have the students draw an outside scene before and after a big wind. (*The Wind Blew* by Hutchins)
- Drop several droplets of paint onto paper. With a straw, blow around the paint to create a picture.
- Find pictures of wind instruments in an encyclopedia or a library book. Explain why these instruments are called "wind" instruments. Demonstrate a musical wind instrument if you can (harmonica, kazoo, etc.). With the teacher's supervision, let the other children experiment with the instrument.
- Draw a funny picture of a very windy day in your town. What tricks would the wind play on you and your friends?
- You are taking a ride in a hot-air balloon high over the land. Draw a picture of what you see from your balloon. Where are you flying? Are you over your own town, or have you traveled to some exotic land? (*The Twenty-One Balloons* by Du Bois)
- Design and decorate your own hot-air balloon using paper, paints, markers, or stickers. (Older students can use an actual balloon and attach a small basket or paper box with string or ribbons.)
- Draw a picture of a face so that, when you turn the picture upside-down, it looks like another, completely different face. Turn the picture back and forth several times while you are drawing it to make sure you get the desired effect.

- You are out on the playground on a beautiful summer day, when suddenly the temperature drops by 50 degrees! Draw a picture of the resulting scene. What strange things would you see on such a day?

- Draw a picture depicting a specific climate (polar region, tropical island, mountains, etc.). Add people to your picture who are dressed inappropriately for the temperature you illustrated. Use various techniques to make your picture appear humorous.

- Make a windmill. You will need a stiff piece of paper (6 inches square); a straight pin with a large, colored head; the casing of an old ballpoint pen; a small piece of an eraser; and a plastic straw or thin dowel. Make a 3-inch cut in each corner of the square from the corner toward the center of the square. Alternating corners, bring four of the eight corners you now have to the center of the square. Push the straight pin through each of these four corners. Then push the pin through the center of the square. Cut a small circle off the pen casing and slip it over the end of the pin. This will help your windmill turn more freely. Push the pin through the straw (or rod). Then push the pin into the eraser to cover the point. Your windmill is now ready for use. You can decorate your windmill before assembling it or put stickers on the finished product.

- Make your own kite using the following instructions:

    You will need one 16-inch and one 24-inch dowel, string, a craft knife, a marker, ribbon, glue, tape, and stiff colored paper. Mark the 16-inch dowel at its center and mark the 24-inch dowel one-third of the way down one end.

    Place the short rod horizontally over the longer rod on the marks, forming a cross. Tie the two sticks together at this point.

    Use the knife to make a notch in each end of the two dowels. (Adult supervision required when using knives.)

    Tie the end of a piece of string around the notch in the top of the kite. Bring the string around the outside of the kite frame, slipping it into each notch. When you are back at the top of the kite, tie the string around the notch to finish off.

    Place the frame, long rod down, on the stiff colored paper. Cut the paper in a diamond shape so that each edge overlaps the kite frame by about 1/2 inch. Cut the corners of the diamond-shaped paper so that they are even with the ends of the dowels.

    Put glue along the edges of the paper and fold each edge over to cover the string of the kite frame. Tie a separate length of string to each end of the short dowel and to the top end of the long dowel. Bring the loose ends of these three strings together and tie them to each other. The knot should be positioned about where the two dowels are tied together. Tie the ball of string that you will use to fly the kite to the knot made when you tied the three strings together.

    Glue a length of ribbon to the bottom of the kite to serve as a tail. To add a little more weight, glue paper bows (or some other design) along the ribbon tail. You can also decorate the kite with colored markers or by gluing paper shapes on it.

Chapter 3
Precipitation

■ Teaching Resources

Books containing experiment(s) relating to the subject matter are marked with a plus sign (+) before and after the title.

P   *The Cloud Book,* by Tomie de Paola (Holiday House, 1985)
Introduces the 10 most common types of clouds and the stories that inspired their names. Also explains the weather that the clouds portend. This book contains very simple reading and explanations. The artist's depictions are childlike in nature.

P   *Down Comes the Rain,* by Franklyn Branley (HarperCollins, 1997)
Explains how the water cycle leads to different types of weather patterns.

P   *Flash, Crash, Rumble, and Roll,* by Franklyn M. Branley (HarperCollins Juvenile Books, 1999)
Explains how and why a thunderstorm occurs. Excellent illustrations with easy-to-understand language. Also gives safety tips on what to do when lightning occurs.

P   *Hurricanes,* by Arlene Erlbach (Children's Press, 1993)
A New True Book that describes the movements and destructive power of hurricanes and explains how they are predicted.

P   *+Hurricanes+,* by Sally Lee (Franklin Watts, 1994)
A discussion of hurricanes, their formation and structure, forecasting, and safety.

P   *Rain,* by Kay Davies and Wendy Oldfield (Raintree Steck-Vaughn, 1995)
Covers a variety of rain topics, such as how clouds make rain, how birds stay dry, and that plants and animals need rain.

P   *Rain,* by Joy Palmer (Raintree Steck-Vaughn, 1994)
Describes rain, how and why it falls, how it can be measured and predicted, and its effects on life.

P   *Rain, Snow, and Ice,* by Ann Merk and Jim Merk (Rourke, 1994)
An introduction to these forms of precipitation.

P   *+Snow Is Falling,+* by Franklyn M. Branley (HarperCollins Juvenile Books, 2000)
Describes the characteristics of snow, its usefulness to plants and animals, and the hazards it can cause.

P   *The Water's Journey,* by Eleonore Schmid (Econo-Clad, 1999)
Simple poetic text and beautiful paintings show the cycle of water, from raindrops flowing to the ocean and back again to a mist.

P   *What Do You See in a Cloud?*, by Allan Fowler (Children's Press, 1996)
Simple text and illustrations describe how clouds differ, what they are made of, and why they turn into rain.

P/ I *Blizzard,* by Christopher Lampton (Millbrook Press, 1994)
Details the development, warning signs, and destructive force of blizzards, as well as self-protection against them.

P/ I *Lightning,* by Peter Murray (Child's World, 1996)
Explains how lightning forms and the impact it can have.

P/ I *Questions and Answers about Weather,* by Jean M. Craig (Scholastic, 1996)
Answers questions about wind, heat, rain, and snow, and looks at weather forecasting methods.

P/ I *Rain,* by Andres Llamas Ruiz (Sterling, 1996)
Provides an introduction to weather phenomena associated with rain.

P/ I *Tornadoes,* by Peter Murray (Child's World, 1996)
An introduction to tornadoes.

P/ I *Weather Everywhere,* by Denise Casey (Macmillan Books for Young Readers, 1995)
Introduction to temperature, wind, and moisture, the three primary elements that create weather conditions.

P/I/U   +*Tornadoes,*+ by Ann Armbruster (Econo-Clad, 1999)
Describes the causes, different parts, and movements of tornadoes. Discusses how they are traced and studied. Includes science projects and safety tips. Excellent photographs and illustrations used to supplement easy-to-read explanations.

I   *Lightning,* by Stephen Kramer (First Avenue Editions, 1993)
Covers a variety of facts on lightning, including how it is formed, the different types of lightning, what thunder is and its relationship to lightning, and safety measures.

I   *Storms,* by Seymour Simon (Mulberry Books, 1992)
Describes the atmospheric conditions that create thunderstorms, hailstorms, lightning, tornadoes, and hurricanes, and explains how violent weather affects the environment and people. Excellent photographs and large print.

I   *Weatherwise: Learning about the Weather,* by Jonathan D. Kahl (Lerner, 1992)
Discusses many aspects of the weather, such as climate and seasons, wind, humidity, clouds, rain, and weather forecasting.

I   *Wild Weather, Hurricanes,* by Lorraine Jean Hopping (Cartwheel Books, 1995)
Discusses where hurricanes come from, what types there are, and what can be done during one.

U *1001 Questions Answered about Hurricanes, Tornadoes, and Other Natural Air Disasters,* by Barbara Tufty (Dover, 1987)
Questions regarding characteristics of storms, weather terms, and natural disasters are answered. Minimal use of photos.

U *The Weather Sky,* by Bruce McMillan (Farrar, Straus & Giroux, 1991)
A study of weather patterns and clouds that occur in the Earth's temperate zones. Contains a good mixture of illustrations and photographs.

■ Reading Selections

Books marked with an asterisk (*) before and after the title are related to activities in the activity sections of this chapter.

Abel's Island, by William Steig (Econo-Clad, 1999)
> Abel's mouse world has always been a secure place to live until flood waters carry him off and dump him on an uninhabited island. (Chapter Book)

Before the Storm, by Jane Yolen (Boyds Mills Press, 1995)
> Story and pictures capture the still moments before a summer storm.

The Big Snow, by Bertha Hader and Elmer Hader (Econo-Clad, 1999)
> Animals are hurrying to prepare for winter. When the big snow arrives, the animals find that the people in one house have left them food. (Available: audiocassette by Weston Woods, 1984.)

The Black Snowman, by Phil Mendez (Scholastic, 1991)
> A piece of African cloth draped over a sooty snowman brings him to life in time to save two brothers from a fire.

Bringing the Rain to Kapiti Plain, by Verna Aardema (Dial Books for Young Readers, 1992)
> A cumulative rhyme relating how Ki-pat brought rain to the drought-stricken Kapiti Plain.

Cloud Nine, by Norman Silver (Clarion Books, 1995)
> It's too noisy at Armstrong's house, so when his dad tells him to go outside, Armstrong builds a ladder to the clouds and finds peace and quiet.

Cloudland, by John Burningham (Crown, 1996)
> While high in the mountains with his parents, Albert falls off a cliff and ends up in Cloudland, where he enjoys playing with the cloud children but he misses his parents.

C.L.O.U.D.S., by Pat Cummings (Lothrop, Lee & Shepard, 1986)
> Chuku is given the job of painting the skies of New York City, an assignment he approaches with reluctance but grows to love.

Cloudy with a Chance of Meatballs, by Judi Barrett (Econo-Clad, 1999)
> Life is delicious in the town of Chewandswallow, where it rains soup and juice, snows mashed potatoes, and blows storms of hamburgers—until the weather takes a turn for the worse.

Come a Tide, by George Ella Lyon (Orchard, 1993)
> Cheerful illustrations depict the doughty neighborliness of rumpled folk as they cope with floodwaters and torrential rains.

Don't Worry, Grandpa, by Nick Ward (Barron's Educational Series, 1995)
> Grandpa gets nervous when a thunderstorm starts, until Charlie explains that storms are caused by giants coming out to play.

First Snow, by Kim Lewis (Candlewick Press, 1996)
> On a trip up the hill with her mother to feed the sheep, a young girl loses her teddy bear when it starts to snow.

Hi, Clouds, by Carol Greene (Children's Press), 1983
> Two children watch clouds become fat and thin, white and gray, then turn into dogs, sheep, dragons, and castles.

Hide and Seek Fog, by Alvin Tresselt (William Morrow, 1987)
> Fog takes over a small village for three days. (Available: audiocassette by Spoken Arts, 1992.)

The House in the Snow, by M. J. Engh (Scholastic, 1990)
> Nine boys outwit the invisible robbers who have inhabited the house in the snow for generations by using the robbers' own cloaks of invisibility. (Chapter Book)

Hurricane, by David Wiesner (Clarion Books, 1990)
> The morning after a hurricane, two brothers find an uprooted tree, which transports them on adventures through their imaginations.

Ice Cream Is Falling!, by Shiegeo Watanabe (Philomel, 1989)
> Bear and his friends have a wonderful time playing when they see snow for the first time.

It Looked Like Spilt Milk, by Charles Shaw (HarperCollins, 1993)
> White images remind the reader of different objects but turn out to be clouds.

The Jacket I Wear in the Snow, by Shirley Neitzel (Mulberry Books, 1994)
> A young girl names all the clothes that she must wear to play in the snow.

Land of the Long White Cloud: Maori Myths, Tales & Legends, by Kiri Te Kanawa (Trafalgar Square, 1997)
> A handsomely illustrated collection of traditional tales provides a glimpse of South Seas magic.

Listen to the Rain, by Bill Martin Jr. and John Archambault (Henry Holt, 1988)
> Describes the changing sounds of the rain: the slow, soft sprinkle, the drip-drop tinkle, the sounding, pounding, roaring rain, and the fresh, wet, silent aftertime of rain. (Poem Form.)

Little Cloud, by Eric Carle (Philomel, 1996)
> A little cloud becomes all sorts of things before joining the other clouds and raining.

The Monster Storm, by Jeanne Willis (Lothrop, Lee & Shepard, 1995)
> A little monster is afraid of a thunderstorm, so he goes outside and tries to scare it away.

On Monday When It Rained, by Cherryl Kachenmeister (Houghton Mifflin, 1989)
> A young boy describes, in text and photographs of his facial expressions, the different emotions he feels each day.

Peter Spier's Rain, by Peter Spier (Picture Yearling Books, 1997)
> Two children play in their backyard on a rainy day. This book contains pictures only.

Rain, by Kirsty Gunn (Grove Press, 1996)
> A family story about brothers and sisters. (Chapter Book)

Rain, by Robert Kalan (Mulberry Books, 1991)
>Brief text and illustrations describe a rainstorm.

Rain, Rain Rivers, by Uri Shulevitz (Farrar, Straus & Giroux, 1988)
>A child indoors watches the rain on the window and in the streets and tells how it falls on the fields, hills, and seas.

Rainy Day Stories and Poems, by Caroline Feller Bauer (J. B. Lippincott, 1987)
>A collection of stories and poems about rain.

Sing, Sophie!, by Dayle Ann Dodds (Candlewick Press, 1997)
>Although no one else in her family likes Sophie's voice, it soothes her baby brother during a thunderstorm.

Snow, by Nancy Elizabeth Wallace (Golden Books, 1999)
>A grown rabbit reminisces about the magic and warmth of the times when he, his brother, and his mother frolicked in the first snowfall of the year.

The Snowy Day, by Ezra Jack Keats (Viking Children's Books, 1996)
>The story of a little boy's adventures in the snow.

Snowy Day Stories and Poems, by Caroline Feller Bauer (J. B. Lippincott, 1986)
>A collection of stories and poems about snow.

Stopping by the Woods on a Snowy Evening, by Robert Frost (E. P. Dutton, 1985)
>A poem describing a winter evening. Includes the well-known passage, ". . . and miles to go before I sleep."

The Storm Book, by Charlotte Zolotow (Harper Trophy, 1989)
>Shows a storm developing and how it affects the country, city, and sea.

Storm in the Night, by Mary Stolz (Harper Trophy, 1990)
>While sitting through a fearsome thunderstorm that has put the lights out, Thomas hears a story from Grandfather's boyhood, when Grandfather was afraid of thunderstorms.

The Sun, the Wind, and the Rain, by Lisa Westberg Peters (Henry Holt, 1990)
>Presents side-by-side narration of the Earth making a mountain, shaping it with sun, wind, and rain, and of a child's efforts at the beach to make a tall sand mountain, which is also affected by the elements.

Thunder Cake, by Patricia Polacco (Paper Star, 1997)
>How a clever grandmother helps her granddaughter overcome her fear of thunderstorms is told in lively pictures and engaging text.

Thunderstorm, by Nathaniel Tripp (Dial Books for Young Readers, 1994)
>As Ben bales the freshly cut hay on his farm and the animals hunt for food for their young, the right weather conditions create a raging thunderstorm that moves swiftly toward them.

Time of Wonder, by Robert McCloskey (Viking, 1989)
>An island family prepares for a hurricane and explores the aftermath.

A Winter Journey, by David Updike (Prentice-Hall, 1985)
>Homer goes out at night into a snowstorm in search of his dog, Sophocles, and experiences some strange and thrilling adventures.

The following books are out of print, but may be available at the local library.

City Storm, by Mary Jessie Parker (Scholastic, 1990
> A chorus of schoolgirls in a city park scurry for shelter when it begins to rain and gleefully watch the sun come back out.

First Snow, by Emily Arnold McCullly (Harper & Row, 1985)
> A timid, little mouse discovers the thrill of sledding in the first snowfall of winter. (No words.)

It Chanced to Rain, by Kathleen Bullock (Simon & Schuster, 1989)
> Out for a walk, Ms. Pig's class gets caught in the rain. Not everyone is upset.

Jonathan's Cloud, by Gardner McFall (Harper & Row, 1986)
> Jonathan wants to keep the cloud that floats into his room, but he doesn't know how to take care of it.

Rain Talk, by Mary Serfozo (Macmillan, 1990)
> A child enjoys a glorious day in the rain, listening to the varied sounds it makes as it comes down.

The Same Wind, by Bette Killion (HarperCollins, 1992)
> A little girl asks the wind that is blowing her curtains if he is the same wind that can sail a boat or form a tornado.

Snow Party, by Beatrice Schen de Regniers (Lothrop, Lee & Shepard, 1989)
> On a snowy, windy night at a Dakota farm, a lonely woman wishes for company, music, and a party. Suddenly, all of her wishes start to come true.

That Sky, That Rain, by Carolyn Otto (Thomas Y. Crowell, 1990)
> As a rainstorm approaches, a young girl and her grandfather take the farm animals into the shelter of the barn and then watch the rain begin.

Thunderstorm, by Mary Szilagyi (Bradbury Press, 1985)
> A little girl is comforted by her mother during a thunderstorm and, in turn, comforts her dog.

Tornado!, by Hilary Milton (Franklin Watts, 1983)
> Stranded on the road by a flood and tornadoes, his mother wounded, and his seven-year-old sister in desperate need of medical attention as the result of a snakebite, 14-year-old Paul exhibits heroism and resourcefulness. (Chapter Book)

Willy Whyner, Cloud Designer, by Michael and Esther Lustig (Four Winds Press, 1994)
> Third-grader Willy Whyner turns his interest in clouds into a profitable business when he invents a way to create customized advertising clouds.

■ Science Activities

Precipitation Around the World

As a class, focus on three or four areas of the world (Europe, Asia, Alaska, etc.). Determine the amount of snow and rain each area normally receives. Have the students look up the areas of the world that have the lowest and the highest amounts of precipitation. Discuss possible reasons why these areas have the amounts of precipitation they do.

Precipitation in the United States

- Show the class a map of the United States and ask them: Which states get the most snow? Which probably get no snow?

- Ask the students to discover why someone living on one side of the Great Lakes gets more snow than someone living on the other side?
- Have the students find out if there are states that receive more rain than others, and if so, why.

Precipitation on Kapiti Plain

Have the students read *Bringing the Rain to Kapiti Plain* by Aardema, then ask them these questions: What is the climate of Kenya, Africa like? What is the average rainfall and temperature? How do the plains of Africa compare to the plains of the United States?

Precipitation and Graphs

One method of recording precipitation is to graph it. Have students collect data on your area and then graph it. Listed below are several suggestions on how to set up graphs on precipitation:

- Graph One:

    Prepare a bar graph that shows rainfall, in inches, vertically, and years horizontally.

    Have the students graph fictional data for a 10-year period.

    In which year did the area receive the most rain?

    In which year did the area receive the least rain?

    What is the average rainfall?

- Graph Two:

    Prepare a line graph that shows rainfall, in inches, vertically, and years horizontally. Choose different colors to represent two different cities and graph fictional data for a 5-year period.

    In which year(s) did city 1 receive more rain than city 2?

    In which year(s) did city 1 receive less rain than city 2?

    Which city received the most rain over a 5-year period?

- Graph Three:

    Prepare a bar graph that shows snowfall, in inches, vertically, and days of a specific month horizontally. Pick a northern city for which data are easily accessible and graph the snowfall for a specific period of time.

    On what day did the city get the most snow?

    How many days did it not snow?

    On what days did it snow more than two inches?

    On what days did it snow one inch?

    What was the total snowfall?

Evidencing Evaporation and Condensation at Home

Ask the students to be science sleuths and look for other examples of evaporation and condensation in their houses:

- After a shower, examine the bathroom for condensation. Later, notice that the wet towels have dried.

- Look for condensation and evaporation when cooking and when serving beverages.
- Breathe on a mirror. What happens?
- Your mother or father is drying his or her hair after a shower. What does he or she use? Why?

Demonstrate Condensation

Demonstrate condensation to the class as follows: Fill a glass with ice cubes and then add water and a drop of food coloring to the ice. Wait 10 minutes. Ask the students: Where did the water on the glass come from? Did it come from inside the glass? How do you know?

Stove-Top Evaporation and Condensation

Ask students to do this experiment at home, with adult supervision. Pour one cup of water into a saucepan. Heat the water to boiling. What is happening to the water? Where is the water going? Hold a lid over the pan. Where is the water coming from that forms on the lid?

Factors That Affect the Rate of Evaporation

Perform the following experiments as a class:

- Measure some water; pour it onto a plate. Measure an equal amount of water; pour it into a tall glass. Ask the students which one evaporates faster, and why.
- Add a teaspoon of cooking oil to one glass and ask the students how the oil affected evaporation.
- Place a saucer with a small amount of water in the sunlight and another saucer with an equal amount of water in a shady place. Have the students identify which one evaporates faster and explain why.
- On two paper towels, place a small amount of water. Fan one towel back and forth. Ask the students which towel dried faster, and why.
- Ask students to do this experiment at home: Put equal amounts of water on two paper towels. Put one towel in the bathroom while someone takes a hot shower and the other towel on the kitchen table. Which evaporates faster? Why?

Fog and Geography

Show the class a map of the San Francisco area and then of London, England. Discuss what makes these areas so foggy. What do these cities have in common that might affect their climate? (Additional information can be obtained from an encyclopedia.)

Weather Charts

Have students make weather charts on paper. They should draw a box for each day of the week, similar to a calendar, then record the presence or absence of clouds each day and what type of clouds they are. Ask them to note whether any precipitation occurred each day. Can they discover whether there is a correlation between the types of clouds observed and the presence or absence of rain or snow?

Cloud Watching

Take the class outside to spend some time watching the clouds. Discuss the shapes the students find in them. Ask them if the shapes change while you are watching them, and if so, why that happens.

Clouds and Math

Review math problems by making a cloud worksheet. Draw several clouds, and on each cloud write a math problem that correlates to what the students are presently studying. After students have completed the worksheet, have them draw their own cloud worksheets. Instruct them to fill in their clouds with the math problems and give the sheets to other students to solve.

Hurricanes and Their Effects

Study the effects of a hurricane. Ask the students to research the following questions: How much damage did Hurricane Andrew do? Hurricane Iliki? What precautions can one take when expecting a hurricane? Find and read to the class stories of unique ways in which people protected themselves and thus survived a hurricane. Discuss why they succeeded.

Locations of Tornadoes

Have the students find out where "Tornado Alley" is and answer these questions: What types of landforms and climates are susceptible to tornadoes? Where have the biggest/worst tornadoes hit? Where are hurricanes prevalent?

Rate, Distance, and Speed Calculations

Ask the students questions regarding the speed of a moving storm and predicting when it will reach your town. For example, if a storm is traveling 30 mph toward your city and it is 120 miles away, how long will it take to reach you? (Answer: 4 hours.)

Making a Tornado

Have the students make a tornado by filling a jar with water and adding a pinch of salt and two or three drops of dishwashing liquid, screwing the lid on tightly, and swirling the jar. They will be able to watch the tornado form.

Tornado Safety

As a class, write a list of safety rules and procedures to follow during a tornado. Have them post the list inside a cabinet door at home for easy access. Information can be obtained by reading books on tornadoes, writing to a weather agency for safety procedures, or calling the local radio or television station.

Make Your Own Lightning

Ask students to try this experiment at home: While wearing leather-soled shoes, shuffle your feet across a carpet and then touch a metal doorknob. The spark you see is created in the same way that lightning is. The energy created is quickly released and is easily carried by the moisture in the air.

Grounding

Students may have heard that a person is safe in a car during an electrical storm even if it is hit by lightning. Have them research why this is so.

Be Prepared

Ask the class to pretend that a blizzard has been forecasted for your town. Once the snowstorm arrives, you expect everyone to be housebound for one week, without electricity for much of that time. Have students make a list of things they must do to prepare for the storm. What items would they need to buy to be properly supplied for the ordeal?

Practice Measuring Skills

Read *Thunder Cake* by Polacco to the class, then make Grandma's Thunder Cake. Have the students do the measuring.

Critical Thinking Challenge 1

Ask students to try to determine a method to measure a raindrop. (One method is to place a piece of cardboard out in the rain for 15–30 seconds. The diameter of the spots on the cardboard can be measured.)

Critical Thinking Challenge 2

Ask the students to hypothesize why they feel cold when stepping out of a shower. (As the water evaporates off a body, it requires heat that it takes from the body. When a person dries off, the evaporation process is halted.)

Critical Thinking Challenge 3 (Advanced)

Heat a skillet and add a couple of drops of water to the pan. At some point, the added drops will appear to "dance" around. Ask the students if they can explain why. (The bottom surface of a water drop is evaporating and forming an invisible layer of steam that keeps the water drop from actually touching the metal of the frying pan. The drops roll around on this layer of steam. If the pan is too hot, the drops quickly boil away. If the pan is too cool, the steam forms too slowly and the drops spread out and, again, boil away.)

■ Creative Writing Activities

Following are instructions to give the students for various writing activities.

- Write a story describing a late autumn rain that turned into the first snowfall of the year. How much did it snow? Did you play in it? What happened?
- Read *It Chanced to Rain* by Bullock. Pretend you are caught in the rain. Would you rather warm up inside or play outside? Write a letter to Paula Pig's Boarding School letting Ms. Pig know where to find you if it rains. (More advanced students could write a story about how other animals might react to a sudden rainfall.)
- Read *Rain* by Kalan. Write a book in a similar style, describing a snowfall, beginning with "Blue Sky." Each page can be illustrated using two or three colors, as is done in the illustrations in the book.
- Read *Snow Party* by de Regniers. Write a letter to someone you know who may be lonely.
- Read *First Snow* by McCully. Write a story that goes with the illustrations. (More advanced students could write a book about a mouse on the first day of summer and illustrate it.)
- Have you ever eaten snowflakes? How did they taste? Write a letter to a friend describing how the snow tasted. (*Ice Cream Is Falling!* by Watanabe)

- Make a snow cone by sprinkling a flavored gelatin mix over a cup of clean snow. Write a recipe telling how to make your favorite flavor of snow cone. Write a story about a land where it snows a different flavor each month. Which month is your favorite?

- Pretend a snowman came to life. Spend a day or night with him. What exciting things would you do? Where would you go? How would you feel when he melted; or what would you do to prevent his melting?

- Read *Cloudy with a Chance of Meatballs* by Barrett. Write a similar story using your favorite foods. (When more than one student is involved, make a class book, with each student drawing a picture of a weather condition involving food.)

- Pretend you are on "Cloud 9." Write a story describing what you are doing and feeling. What makes life on Cloud 9 so perfect?

- Go outside and look at the clouds. Write a story describing what you see. How would these clouds look from an airplane?

- Write a story about living in a place that is always foggy. How does it make you feel? What would you name the city? What do the people do to try to "lift" the fog?

- Take an imaginary trip to a city in the clouds. What do the people do there? How do the houses and plants look? What jobs do the people do that are different from jobs here on Earth? How does it feel to walk on the clouds?

- You are visiting another planet and see many strange things. But the strangest of all is the appearance of the clouds. The clouds are not white and fluffy or made of water, but very different. Write a letter to someone at home describing the clouds on this strange planet.

- Finish this story: "Jason stormed into the room. He was so mad! 'You'll never believe what just happened!' he said." What does the word *stormed* mean in this context?

- Write a story in which you are a pioneer settling a new land. Describe how a fierce storm threatens your existence. As a different twist to this exercise, write a story about how a thunderstorm saved your farm.

- Write a story telling how you were brave during a thunderstorm (*Thunderstorm* by Szilagyi).

- What is the difference between a hurricane, a typhoon, a cyclone, and a monsoon? Where is each found? Write an informative article for a magazine as if you were the "science reporter" describing your findings.

- Read *Hurricane* by Wiesner. Pretend you are in the uprooted tree. Where does your imagination take you? Write a story about your adventures.

- Imagine you are a television weather forecaster. Write the script you will use to explain that a hurricane is headed your way. Be sure to tell your viewers what safety precautions to take. You can even create a television studio by hanging a map behind a desk or table. Then videotape your "broadcast" to critique or just to enjoy.

- You are walking along the main street in town when it begins to pour. You run for cover into the nearest shop. It happens to be a new store that you've never seen before. You are amazed at what you discover inside. Write an account about what you discover in this new and unusual store. Would you like to have a job there?

■ Art Activities

Following are instructions to give the students for various art activities.

- Cut out snowflakes from folded paper. Paste them on different-colored construction paper. Try to make the snowflakes with only six sides, like real ones.

- Divide a sheet of paper into two sections. Cut out pictures of clothes and paste them on either the "summer" side or the "winter" side. Arrange the photos in a collage. (*The Jacket I Wear in the Snow* by Neitzel)

- Draw a picture illustrating "raining cats and dogs." What would you like to have "rain" instead of water? Draw a picture of that.

- Sing songs about rain and snow. List any songs you know about rain or snow. How does the rain or snow set the mood of the song? Some songs you may remember are:

  "Raindrops Keep Falling on my Head"

  "Let It Snow"

  "Walking in a Winter Wonderland"

  "Singing in the Rain"

  "Itsy, Bitsy Spider"

  "Frosty the Snowman"

- Make soap snow and create pictures on black construction paper. Soap snow can be made by mixing 1 1/2 cups of white soap flakes with 1cup of hot water. Beat with an eggbeater until stiff.

- Look at photos of people and guess the emotions they are feeling. Draw a picture of your face and how you feel when it rains. Then draw a similar picture of your face when it snows. (*On Monday When It Rained* by Kachenmeister)

- On a piece of paper, draw a "happy" picture of you enjoying the weather (building a snowman, walking in the rain, enjoying a picnic). On the other side of the paper, draw an "unhappy" picture of a time when you did not enjoy the weather.

- Cut out a picture of a farm animal from a magazine and paste it on a piece of paper. Draw a rainy farm scene around the animal. (*That Sky, That Rain* by Otto)

- Draw a winter scene on black construction paper using chalk. (*The Black Snowman* by Mendez)

- Using blue construction paper, white paint, and a sponge, "sponge" clouds onto the paper. What do they look like to you? (*It Looked Like Spilt Milk* by Shaw)

- Read *C.L.O.U.D.S.* by Cummings. Draw a sequence of clouds changing from one form to another, similar to the way the clouds were changed in the book.

- Using cotton balls and blue construction paper, or white paper that you have colored blue, create a picture of the sky. Go outside and observe what the clouds look like at that moment and try to re-create the scene using the cotton and construction paper.

- Draw a picture of fog rolling into your town. How would you draw fog?

- Draw a line across the middle of a piece of paper. On the top half of the paper, draw the clouds you see in the sky. On the bottom half, draw pictures of the objects the clouds remind you of.

- Pretend that you are asked to design the clouds that will be in the sky for one day all over the United States. What different cloud formations would you design for special cities? (For example, you might draw buffalo-shaped clouds over Buffalo, New York; apple-shaped clouds over New York City, the Big Apple; or heart-shaped clouds for Loveland, Ohio.) What would the clouds look like over your own house?

- Create your own "thunderstorm" with the rest of your class. Begin by making light rain (snapping fingers), move on to heavy rain (pounding fists on table), then to winds (blowing sounds), and finally, to thunder (stomping feet). Gradually let the thunder subside, the wind diminish, the heavy rain lighten, and finally the rain stop.

- Use a piece of charcoal or black chalk to make a swirling tornado on paper, or make a colored tornado on a black piece of construction paper. (*Tornado!* by Milton)

- Draw a picture of how you think your neighborhood looks during a thunderstorm. (*Thunderstorm* by Szilagyi)

- Watch the movie *The Wizard of Oz*. Make the following drawings based on this story:

    Draw a picture of your house being carried off to the land of Oz in a tornado. You've landed in Oz. What would you make it look like? What do the people look like? Can you think of a better name for them to fit your "Oz?"

    Make up three friends that you meet on the way to see the Wizard. Draw them in a certain spot during your journey to Oz.

    The villain of the story isn't a witch. Draw a picture showing you and your friends with your "villain."

    How do you finally get back home? Draw a picture showing how you were transported back to your home.

    With some construction paper, bind these pictures into a book.

- If you could choose, what would rain or snow be made of? Draw a picture of a rain or snow storm, giving the rain or snow a different form. Would it rain root beer, or snow candy canes? It's your choice! (*Cloudy with a Chance of Meatballs* by Barrett)

- Write a contradictory story about a storm. For example: "It rained so hard the grass shriveled up and died. The thunder was so loud I could hardly hear it." (The children will have fun reading their nonsensical stories, and they will learn something about opposites, too.)

- Make up a scary story about being lost in a fog. Tell the story to your family or friends. (Older students can put on a play telling the story to younger students.) Make simple puppets from socks, paper bags, or drawings glued to Popsicle sticks and put on a puppet show.

Additional Resources

■ Experiment Books

Upper-level students may be encouraged to go beyond library books and textbooks to research what is currently happening in weather and weather forecasting. One magazine that specifically relates to weather is:

WEATHERWISE
4000 Albemarle St., NW
Washington, D.C. 20016

■ Magazine Articles

Articles about weather that can be found in other magazines are listed here by subject.

Weather

"The Stormy Future of Weather Forecasting," *Popular Science* 237 (September 1991): 78–83.

"Test Your Weather IQ," *Good Housekeeping* 212 (January 1991): 169.

"Weather Forecasting: Your Eyes Can Keep You Dry," *The Mother Earth News* 27 (August/September 1991): 36–39.

"Weather Rhymes and Reasons," *Reader's Digest* 137 (July 1990): 60–62.

"What's Wrong with the Weather?" *Time* 139 (June 15, 1992): 60–61.

The Sun and the Seasons

"Could the Sun Be Warming the Climate?" *Science* 254 (November 1, 1991): 652–653.

"Solar Cycles and Atmospheric Warming," *Sky and Telescope* 83 (May 1992): 489.

"The Spots on the Greenhouse," *Newsweek* 118 (November 18, 1991): 88.

Air, Temperature, and Wind

"The Nutrients Are Blowing in the Wind (The Role of Winds in a Global Ecosystem)," *U.S. News and World Report* 111 (October 14, 1991): 66.

"When the Going Gets Cold (Survival Tactics in Animals)," *National Wildlife* 29 (December 1990/January 1991): 6–10.

"Will Winds Help Cool a Warming World?" *Science News* 138 (October 6, 1990): 217.

"Wind at Work," *Sierra* 75 (November/December 1990): 104–105.

Precipitation

"The Fleeting, Eternal Snowflake," *Reader's Digest* 140 (January 1992): 121.

"The Shape of Rain," *Discover* 11 (April 1990): 18.

"Snow Has Secrets to Tell (Evidence of Climate Change and Possible Global Warming)," *National Wildlife* 30 (December 1991/January 1992): 4–9.

"The Wonder of Snow," *Southern Living* 26 (January 1991): 110.

Clouds and Fog

"Clouds and Temperature," *Country Journal* 17 (September/October 1990): 21–22.

"Clouds Keep Ocean Temperatures Down," *Science News* 139 (May 11, 1991): 303.

"Earth Keeps Its Cool (Effects of Cloud Formation on Global Warming)," *Sea Frontiers* 37 (October 1991): 12–13.

"Eleven Important Cloud Formations and What They Bring," *The Mother Earth News* 127 (August/September 1991): 40–41.

Storms

"What Do You Know about Summer Storms?" *Good Housekeeping* 213 (August 1991): 167.

■ Government Agencies

National Weather Service
1325 East/West Hwy.
Silver Spring, MD 20910
301-713-0689

Soil Conservation Service
P.O. Box 2890
Washington, D.C. 20013

■ Web Sites

The following Web sites reference additional Web sites relating to weather. All sites were accessed in March 2001 and were active at that time.

The Weather Channel: http://www.weather.com/
USA Today Weather: http://www.usatoday.com/weather/wfront.htm
WeatherNet: http://cirrus.sprl.umich.edu/wxnet/
Hurricanes: http://www.met.fsu.edu/explores/tropical.html
Rainbow Maker: http://www.zianet.com/rainbow/
Shuttle Observations of Lightning: http://www.ghcc.msfc.nasa.gov/skeets.html
Storm Chaser: http://www.stormchaser.com
National Severe Storms Laboratory: http://www.nssl.noaa.gov/
"Weather Dude": http://wxdude.com
Rainbows: http://www.unidata.ucar.edu/staff/blynds/rnbw.html
Exploring Weather: http://www.exploratorium.edu/weather
Lightning: http://www.nationalgeographic.com/modules/lightning/1.html

Experiments on Thunder: http://www.beakman.com/thunder/thunder.html
National Geophysical Data Center: http://www.ngdc.noaa.gov/
Wild Weather: http://dailynews.yahoo.com/fc/yahooligans/wild_weather
Forecasts and Weather Maps: http://www.yahooligans.com/science_and_nature/the_earth/weather/
     forecasts_and_weather_maps/

Index

About the Authors

Amy J. Bain is a teacher in the Miami Elementary School system, Milford, Ohio, and is president of Solomon Publishing. **Janet Richer** has worked extensively writing and presenting training workshops and videos for homeschooling families throughout the Midwest. **Janet Weckman** is a teacher at Blanche Moore Elementary School, Corpus Christi, Texas, with more than 20 years of teaching experience, including working with hearing-impaired students.

from ***Teacher Ideas Press***

CELEBRATING THE EARTH: Stories, Experiences, Activities
Norma J. Livo

Invite young readers to observe, explore, and appreciate the natural world through engaging activities. Livo shows you how to use folk stories, personal narrative, and a variety of learning projects to teach students about amphibians, reptiles, mammals, constellations, plants, and other natural phenomena. Designed to build a Naturalist Intelligence in young learners, these stories and activities are packed with scientific information. **All Levels.**
xvii, 174p. 8½x11 paper ISBN 1-56308-776-6

FAMOUS PROBLEMS AND THEIR MATHEMATICIANS
Art Johnson

Why did ordering an omelet cost one mathematician his life? The answer to this and other questions are found in this exciting new resource that shows your students how 60 mathematicians discovered mathematical solutions through everyday situations. These lessons are easily incorporated into the curriculum as an introduction to a math concept, a homework piece, or an extra challenge. Teacher notes and suggestions for the classroom are followed by extension problems and additional background material. **Grades 5–12.**
xvi, 179p. 8½x11 paper ISBN 1-56308-446-5

SCIENCE AND MATH BOOKMARK BOOK: 300 Fascinating, Fact-Filled Bookmarks
Kendall Haven and Roni Berg

Use these 300 reproducible bookmarks of fascinating facts, concepts, trivia, inventions, and discoveries to spark student learning. They cover all major disciplines of math and physical, earth, and life sciences—ready to copy, cut out, and give to your students. **Grades 4 and up.**
xii, 115p. 8½x11 paper ISBN 1-56308-675-1

WRITE RIGHT! Creative Writing Using Storytelling Techniques
Kendall Haven

Haven's breakthrough approach to creative writing uses storytelling techniques to enhance the creative writing process. This practical guide offers you directions for 38 writing exercises that will show students how to create powerful and dynamic fiction. All the steps are included, from finding inspiration and creating believable characters to the final edit. Activities are coded by levels, but most can be adapted to various grades. **All Levels.**
240p. 8½x11 paper ISBN 1-56308-677-8

VISUAL MESSAGES: Integrating Imagery into Instruction
2d Edition
David M. Considine and Gail E. Haley

The authors provide effective media literacy strategies, activities, and resources that help students learn the critical-viewing skills necessary in our media-dominated world. Various media and types of programs are addressed, including motion pictures, television news, and advertising. Activities are coded by grade level and curriculum area. **Grades K–12.**
xxiii,371p. 8½x11 paper ISBN 1-56308-575-5

For a free catalog or to place an order, please contact:
Teacher Ideas Press
Dept. B051 • P.O. Box 6633 • Englewood, CO • 80155-6633
800-237-6124 • www.lu.com/tip • Fax: 303-220-8843